BEACH HOUSE HAPPY

COASTAL LIVING

ANTONIA VAN DER MEER

BEACH HOUSE HAPPY

THE JOY OF LIVING BY THE WATER

Oxmoor House®

Contents

FOREWORD

A beach house is a state of mind. It's an antidote to your everyday life. At a beach house there is no traffic, all your gadgets work (and are fully charged), and you never have to go to the dentist—at least, that's the beach house in my mind.

The reality can be a bit different from the fantasy. Real life kinda follows you wherever you go. It's inescapable. My rad retreat on Shelter Island requires a three-hour stress-fest on the legendary Long Island Expressway. My reward for the schlep? The cable is busted, the toilet needs fixing, the freezer was left open …

But there are moments—sometimes entire weekends!—when the fantasy meets the reality. The water is turquoise, and the sky is turquoise-ier. The temperature is unnoticeable. I've had perfect weekends when all of the mosquitoes seem to be on vacation. Sometimes when I hop on my paddleboard in the Peconic Bay, the swells are swell, the clouds are cotton balls, and, if I'm super-duper lucky, I paddle up to a seal. Euphoria.

No matter what greets me at my beach house, it's always a great time to immerse myself in *Beach House Happy*. This magical tome delivers just what it promises. I open the pages, and the sun shines. Traffic? What traffic? I'm on a fluffy sofa, the water is sparkling, I can smell the sea. *Beach House Happy* feels just like a paddleboarding rendezvous with my favorite seal.

This beautiful book is my new happy place. Dive in!

—Jonathan Adler

INTRODUCTION

I WAS BORN ABOUT 1,000 FEET FROM THE WATER. THIS MEANS THAT one of the first sounds I heard in my life, besides my mother cooing at me, would have been the low moan of a foghorn from one of the two working lighthouses nearby. And the first scent I might have noticed would have been the salt air as soon as I left the hospital with my parents. Once my eyes adjusted to the light and my surroundings, one of my earliest views would have been of the water, because we lived on a small cove. By the time I was 5, we had moved even closer to the beach, just across the street from the ocean, and my fate was sealed. I was a water baby from the very beginning; the sea was in my blood from the get-go.

I am guessing that because you picked up this book, you feel that way, too. Water has a magnetic power for people. "Nothing will content [us] but the extremest limit of the land," Herman Melville writes in *Moby-Dick*. He's right. We have all seen this: People are invariably drawn straight to the ends of piers, to the edges of cliffs, to the rims of tide pools. They "must get just as nigh the water as they possibly can without falling in," Melville says. This always makes me laugh, especially because I often can be found hanging over the railing of ferries, inching my way to the edge of a cliff walk, or climbing out onto a rock to get closer to the water.

Some of the earliest photographs I have seen of myself as a child were taken at the beach in front of my grandparents' house. In one in particular (I am about 3 years old, I think), I am sitting with my mother and my grandmother on a rock jetty—because, as Melville has made so clear, we need to get close enough to risk falling in. It wasn't long afterward that I was properly taught to swim. My grandfather, a wonderfully gentle and generous man, made it his personal mission to teach me. He loved the water, and swam in the sea every day that the weather allowed. I remember being shown how to do a dead man's float with my face in the water. There was no fear, only a desire to please my grandfather and to learn to love what he loved. Yes, there was seaweed, and the water in the Northeast can be quite dark, but I concentrated on the surface instead: the beautiful light sparkling on the water, the warm sun on my back, the white sails of a small boat in the distance that had moved a little further away every time my head popped up. And, of course, there was also the thought of warming up later in his house across the street with my grandmother's good cooking in front of me.

My love of the water, and my desire to keep it in my sights, has never waned. I am lucky enough to have a house now in the same area where I grew up. Every time I drive around a bend in the road, and the water comes into view, I feel a sense of happiness and serenity. There it is! It's as though I have never seen it before. In truth, every time it is slightly new. The water changes color as the clouds move into new formations, casting shadows and deepening the blues here and there. When I am near the water, I breathe more deeply. Whatever workaday notion that might have been rattling around in my head sits still, and I am forced to take note of the ocean's beauty before I can move on to anything else.

It is not surprising to me that the Persians held the sea holy, and that the Greeks felt it important enough to give it a separate deity. That love of the water is the cornerstone of every beach house. Even people who don't live near the sea often decorate their homes as though they do, because the colors and themes of the ocean nourish us all. As the editor-in-chief of *Coastal Living,* I have a front-row seat to the types of houses and settings that cannot help but brighten one's day. The photographs we include in every issue of the magazine—of pastel bedrooms,

all-white kitchens, inviting Dutch doors opening out to breezy porches, roof decks with commanding views, and living rooms with cheerful blue-and-white striped rugs—have a feel-good quality. I know this because we receive countless notes from our readers thanking us for bringing rays of summer sunshine into their lives even during the cold winter months.

During my time at the magazine, I have found myself thinking more and more about how happiness is inexorably tied to the beach and to the beach house (or any house near enough to the water to borrow that title). A beautiful collection of blue sea glass bottles sitting on a shelf, with the light hitting it just so, draws the eye and sparks the imagination. A quiet nook with a comfortable chair and a cashmere throw calls out for a long, contented sit-down with a good book. A bedroom window that has a late-afternoon view of shimmering water with a sailboat gliding by says stop, look, breathe. A kitchen with shelving painted a Caribbean blue does double duty: displaying cookware for the preparation of food but also adding a visual invitation to enjoy it. A white denim slipcovered sofa encourages you to have a real, intimate conversation because you just don't want to get up. Within beach houses, there is so much beauty to be found, so many opportunities for relaxation, recuperation, and restoration.

Of course we cannot always be happy when at a beach house. Life ticks on there as elsewhere, with its challenges and its occasional heartaches. But the location and architecture of a beach house, along with the things that fill it, contribute mightily to a sense of well-being, hope, healing, and joy. And that is what I most want to explore in this book.

I am not the first person to notice the effect that a house can have on happiness. Alain de Botton does a wonderful job of explaining the compelling connection between buildings and people in his book, *The Architecture of Happiness*. In it, he argues that a home provides "not only physical but also psychological sanctuary," and suggests that we "open ourselves to the idea that we are affected by our surroundings." Architecture and interior design can combine to make a distinct contribution to our overall happiness.

Amusingly, he points out that we also must concede that "we are inconveniently vulnerable to the colour of our wallpaper and that our sense of purpose may be derailed by an unfortunate bedspread." I have to laugh, but I also have decided to use this logic as an excuse to buy some lovely new things for my home, lest my sense of purpose find itself so unfortunately derailed. Barring that, however, happiness in a beach house is not tied to buying things. So many of the beach houses we love are small, simple, and decidedly worn around the edges. They contain beloved seashell collections, children's artwork, and chipped antiques. In my own beach house, I often have noted that I find a sticky door, a recalcitrant lock, or an uneven step endearing.

The beauty of a beach house does not come from dramatic, fanciful, or over-the-top elements. Instead it comes from a humbler, deeper place. A beach house is like a well from which we draw memories of the happy times spent there; it is the reserve we tap when we need to recharge and relax. Happiness in our homes is tied to the little things: the oak banister on the second floor that you lean over when shouting downstairs, a collection of vintage postcards that lines a shelf in the study, the cabinets in the butler's pantry that are full of your favorite tea and cookies, or the sconces in the entry hall that cast a warm glow at night. We walk by these things every day, and each one (when it is just right) gives us a little extra energy, that jolt of happiness that propels us through our days.

There were so many great photographs I could have shared with you in this book. Beach houses are comfortable spaces for families and friends, and they exude a particular warmth and beauty that is not often found anywhere else. So it was hard to choose. But after looking through all the amazing houses we have published over the past five years, I narrowed it down to the ones that I thought have that surge of happy energy. At the same time, I began to research happiness. Where does it come from? What makes us happy? Are there ways to increase our happiness? How do our surroundings add to feelings of joy? I discovered that many of the things that are scientifically and empirically tied to happiness are abundant in beach houses: balance, color, history, sharing, surprise, and nature. Let's take a quick look at each one.

BALANCE A happy life is a balanced life, where there is time for work and time for play, moments for reflection and moments for interacting with others. In balance we find order and respite from an increasingly hectic world. The best beach houses achieve this through quiet, uncluttered design and help us unwind, relax, and experience a sense of restfulness in our lives.

COLOR Much research has been done regarding color's effect on the human psyche. Those results have even been used to sell products; many of the items in a grocery store are bright red or yellow, proven happy attention-getters. Blue, the color we most often associate with the beach, is a clear winner when it comes to de-stressing people. In beach houses, we see a rainbow of strong, bright colors, from orange to turquoise. We seem almost fearless about color at the beach, where it appears so natural to be our happiest selves.

HISTORY Homes with history are like old friends; they know all our stories, and they nurture us. Being connected to the past strengthens us and makes us feel happier about where we are now. Without respect for what came before, we can easily become unmoored and feel unprepared for the future. Tradition feeds our souls. Some of the older beach communities are wonderful examples of the ways in which history grounds us and makes us feel part of a larger whole.

SHARING It is the rare study of happiness that does not mention the benefits of generosity. When we share, our sense of joy is greatly enhanced. The old saying "it is better to give than to receive" is more a fact than an adage. And where is generosity more apparent than at a beach house, where family, neighbors, and friends are always welcome? Open spaces, big porches, and comfortable decor all enhance our ability to share our beach homes with others.

SURPRISE Pleasant surprises lead to joy. Beach houses almost always come through on that score; they are often filled with exciting and special touches such as airy staircases, stenciled patterns on floors, and whimsical collectibles. And the beach itself is full of surprises on any given day—an extra-large wave that crashes at your feet, or a perfect piece of sea glass winking at you from the sand.

NATURE Nature has long been linked to elevated moods. At the beach, the sound of the waves and the feeling of the sand beneath our feet can help the stress of everyday life fall away. Reconnecting with the great outdoors is the best boost for our outlook on life in general. The beach house, by its very location, is an agent of nature, and a key place for getting back in touch with the environment. The water, shells, dunes, beach stones, sea grass—each one speaks to us and soothes the soul. Houses that connect us to nature boast well-used outdoor living areas, grand views, and organic materials inside and out.

As I worked on this book, the people I interviewed spoke about all of these things, and told me how each one of these qualities contributes to their happiness in their homes. Common themes popped up, including the idea that beach homes have the ability and the power to physically and spiritually heal us, as well as relax us and make us happier people. In fact, most people spoke to me about their beach house as if it were a child or a dear friend. The emotional connection to these homes is so strong that they seem to take on human attributes.

I refer to my own house as having a personality, too: stalwart and patient. Like many people with homes on or near the coast, we are not there full-time. So my house, unfortunately, needs to wait its turn for attention and love. Summer and weekend homes may not hear footsteps for weeks, only to be overrun suddenly by the noise and chaos of boisterous children, the sound of a broom moving the sand back out the door, the smell and the smoke of a late-night barbecue, the constant whir of the outdoor shower and the washing machine. These houses wait for us. Mine has lasted through time and turmoil—and even hurricanes. Many others in this book have, as well.

There is an intense attachment to properties near the water. One homeowner told me that she could sell her primary residence without shedding a tear, but her beach house is a property she wants to keep forever. I can relate. Mine is the house where I grew up, and it is now our weekend house. It's the place my children spent every summer—swimming to the raft, running along the beach, digging in the sand. I hope that any future grandchildren will eventually follow, and that the house will continue to play an important role in the lives of a new generation.

The beach house is not just a happy place; it is a forever place. Let's explore all the ways it captures this magic, and all the ways we can feel beach house happy. ∎

BALANCE

Upon entering a luxury spa, we tend to slow down, breathe more deeply, and speak more quietly. There are physical cues in spas that help us to modify our behavior: ambient lighting, neutral palettes, quiet music, the sound of running water. Spas are designed to reduce stress. Well-designed homes can do this, too, and beach houses seem particularly well suited to the task. Those that exude balance and harmony make us feel at peace with ourselves and can bring about a meditative state that has been associated with increased long-term happiness.

Slowing our thoughts down and taking time away from the constant stimuli of the world can be very beneficial. The act of quiet meditation has become more popular because of its association with positive feelings. Many high-powered individuals practice it to counter the stress in their lives. Those of us who live near the water practice it every day without even thinking—I have often noted how easy it is to spend hours simply staring out at the sea from a beach chair!

In this chapter, a temple-like home in Mexico is a perfect example of a balanced retreat, with its focus on the Caribbean just outside. A home in Florida has clean, uncluttered spaces and white furniture, and soothes you like a glass of white wine at sunset. And a beach house in South Africa succeeds by not trying hard to impress. Instead, it keeps a low profile, doing nothing to distract you from its beautiful setting, or from your own inner thoughts.

Balance and harmony are keys to a more peaceful, less stressful world, one that ultimately delivers the continued gift of happiness.

A SACRED PLACE
Puerto Aventuras, Mexico

THE RIVIERA MAYA ON THE YUCATÁN PENINSULA in Mexico is a mystical and magical area, where true harmony with nature seems not only possible but downright unavoidable. With the famous ruins of Tulum found here, the very land appears to be sacred. The remaining structures include a temple with mysterious murals and carvings depicting Mayan gods—including a diving god. The ancient civilization has long been an object of wonder because of its impressive accomplishments: a complex system of numbers and mathematical calculations, an ability to navigate the sea, and the creation of a calendar. What better place for a balanced and spiritual beach house than in nearby Puerto Aventuras, where Jim and Viola Delameter's home sits majestically on the rocks? With sweeping views of the Caribbean, it looks like a temple dedicated to the sun, sea, and sky.

This tranquil and airy vibe springs in large part from the Delameters' love of Mexican architecture, specifically that of architect Luis Barragán. Barragán is known for his clean, modern lines but he was not really a classic minimalist. Instead, he was a proponent of "emotional architecture" and has been quoted as saying, "Any work of architecture which does not express serenity is a mistake." He almost always worked with stone and wood as his raw materials. Using this same notion, the Delameters have created a home that is a clear example of the ways in which architecture can express serenity. In a nod to Barragán's style, the home is designed to resemble a basic glass-and-concrete box. The structure is almost primitive in feel, with a practical simplicity. But there is a light, open quality, because the home is built around a courtyard

with Italian-style loggias on the first floor. The ceilings are 14 feet high to provide the house with as much light as possible. As you approach the glass front door, you can see straight through to the Caribbean Sea—an open invitation to enter a world of peace and harmony.

A lap pool runs alongside the house, opening into the larger pool area facing the sea. Two of the four bedrooms face the ocean and share a wide porch, perfect for lazy afternoons overlooking the Caribbean. "It's simple and sunny, with an inside/outside feel. There are open spaces everywhere," says Jim. Therein lies its charm. The openness allows it to remain in harmony with the low jungle around it and the ocean view in front of it. The result is a home that exerts a calming influence and helps the mind to rest.

The interiors are designed to be as carefree as possible. There is a softness about this home and, despite all of the cool concrete and limestone, there is a warmth. Everything feels well worn and balanced, thanks to furnishings such as the plain wooden table and slatted chairs on the upstairs balcony, or the two matching barrel-shaped leather chairs, slipcovered in linen, in the living area. Nothing is shiny or new here; there are no jarring colors. The palette used throughout is gray, white, and brown, so as not to compete with the lush greens and cobalt blues outside. Restful and quiet, the neutral fabrics and furnishings all look as though they have been faded by the sun over the years. The furnishings were almost all locally sourced, meaning that they fit in perfectly with the area. The beauty of this place touches the soul.

Jim's goal was to keep the retreat as simple as possible, and he has succeeded in creating a peaceful atmosphere, unencumbered by any visual noise. With less in the house

OPPOSITE: A few large green palm fronds placed in a clear glass vase create a quiet still life, as beautiful as a work of art. A simple leather-bound journal reminds one of how precious it is to find the time for collected thoughts.

to worry about, stress is immediately reduced. The decor is minimal—there are no knickknacks, ornate architectural elements, or unnecessary flourishes. Instead, the simplest of items can become decorative. A handmade ladder, for example, became an *objet d'art* after it was left behind by the workers who built the house. The homeowners loved it and fought to save it from being thrown out. It is just pieces of wood nailed together, but it takes on an almost philosophical air and looks beautiful resting against the concrete side of the house, next to the azure lap pool.

Jim tells me that he built the house with the environment in mind. He chose to build on the rocks rather than on the beach because he wanted a protected position—plus it prevents sand from getting into the house. The dwelling can stand up to whatever Mother Nature dishes out: harsh sun, big waves, floodwaters—even hurricanes. At the same time, it is brazenly open to the elements. The entry, courtyard, and staircase have no roof. Jim tells me that during heavy rains he has seen a stream run down the steps, through the living room, into the pool, and then out to the ocean. But he seems amused, not alarmed. The goal was to allow storms to pass through the house, as they would through the rocks along the shore. Much of what washes up is later used as decoration in the house; bleached driftwood is a favorite.

When the Delameters stay here, distractions are few, and fond memories are many. Achieving balance is a happy result of the home's architecture. The Greek philosopher Euripides said, "The best and safest thing is to keep a balance in your life, acknowledge the great powers around us and in us. If you can do that and live that way, you are really a wise man." By this measure, the Delameters are wise indeed.

LEFT: The view from this vacation home on the Riviera Maya is spellbinding. The open, curved staircase creates a perfect nook for collected driftwood, instantly elevating it from storm debris to artful objects.

OPPOSITE: The concrete-slab table in the courtyard is from central Mexico. The house has very little artwork in it, and instead makes use of large statement mirrors to dress the space. Woven baskets and clay bowls hold everyday necessities.

ABOVE: There is no better place to sit down for a midday repast than at a rustic wood table on a cool, shaded terrace overlooking the brilliant blue sea. A traditional cotton rope hammock hangs in the corner for afternoon naps.

OPPOSITE: Sleek black iron tables punctuate either end of a trim white sofa, giving definition to the living room. The palette is subdued and restful, allowing the burnished background of the painting above the sofa to pop. The barrel-back chairs are covered in linen and authentically Mexican.

ABOVE: A dramatic four-poster black iron bed is softened by the all-white bedding and pile of plush pillows. Two antique suitcases stacked at the foot of the bed add an element of authenticity to the room. A line of empty wire birdcages in the window subtly reminds you to let your thoughts fly free.

OPPOSITE: The pool looks straight out at the ocean, with all its intense beauty. A few wooden chaises provide space for comfortable sunning. Better yet, when the sea beckons, the homeowners can walk past the wall and enter a protected swimming hole (next page) carved into the lava-like rocks.

BALANCE IS FOUND IN THE RISE AND FALL OF
THE SEA, THE PUSH AND PULL OF THE SUN AND MOON, AND THE
SIMPLE BEAUTY OF A HOUSE BY THE WATER

QUIET TIMES

Plettenberg Bay, South Africa

BEACH HOUSES ARE AT THEIR BEST WHEN THEY exemplify the simple life. Homes in harmony with the surroundings, that don't try too hard to impress, often achieve a Zen-like state that affirms our feelings of serenity in profound ways. Living in a pared-down environment helps restore balance. Have you ever noticed how wonderful it feels to clean out a closet or a desk that has become overburdened with books, photos, papers, and random cords? Suddenly your space is less chaotic, and stress is held at bay. When unnecessary objects have been stripped away, and there are fewer distractions, I find that I want to stay and enjoy it. Sweeping away the clutter allows for contented solitude; I can think clearly again. That's why I find myself so drawn to this beach house, in the coastal town of Plettenberg Bay in South Africa: Its clean, understated style, combined with its incredible seaside location, encourages a meditative state.

Looking at it, I marvel at the minimalist, contemporary approach to a dramatic setting. The boxy, three-story structure is perched like a unique tree house and designed for easy living, which homeowners Frances and Wotjek Orzechowski say makes them feel closer to nature. On one side it faces a bird sanctuary, and the sounds of the singing mix with the sounds of the ocean, just two minutes away across a series of wooden walkways. I can see that the Orzechowskis have worked hard not to make their house a distraction, but rather to give play to everything that lies beyond: the dunes of Robberg Beach, and the wonderful sea and wildlife to be found there.

Designed by South African architect Tessa van Schaik, the house is built of stone and wood, primarily Oregon pine salvaged from a home that was being demolished. There is local pine, too, and blackwood trees, a sustainable choice the couple felt good about. The wood was left to look natural—no stains, varnishes, or paints—so it's perfect under bare feet and, after years of use, has weathered beautifully. "Wood has a natural feeling," Frances tells me. "It feels very soft around us." The flat roof is corrugated tin, not only practical but soothing. When it rains, the drops bounce off in a magical, comforting rhythm, bringing the family even closer to nature. Local stone composes the retaining walls, one of which is now a climbing wall for the Orzechowskis' son, age 15. "We didn't quite know what to do with the retaining wall until my son came up with this idea," Frances admits. Brilliant. I love things that do double duty and that have a sense of fun.

The architecture was inspired and informed by New Zealand's bach-style bungalows—small, spare, unimposing, and meant to maximize beach time. With that in mind, spaces flow easily from the inside out, with sliding glass doors that open wide for access to the surroundings. The decor also emphasizes the idea of unpretentious, straightforward living and an open-air atmosphere. The focused minimalism of the design and the addition of efficient built-ins are the keys to the family's happiness here. Frances wanted a house created for the way she lives. "It's easy to keep it neat and not gather clutter, because there is no space for it!" she tells me.

Out went all of the things Frances felt the family didn't need: carpets on the floors, heavy treatments on the windows, excessive accessories or collectibles. Here,

OPPOSITE: The box-like structure made of wood and stone reminds me of a stack of children's building blocks—pleasing in its simplicity. It maintains a subdued profile in a peaceful bay area here in South Africa, where untamed nature rules.

quiet reigns, and books are read. A window seat in a sunny corner begs for a cup of tea and some good old-fashioned daydreaming. On chilly nights, the wood-burning stove in the sitting room becomes the center of family activity. The pendant lights inside are made of wood, and cast a soft glow as the sun goes down. A wall of books is the only real decoration in the family room. In other areas of the house, there are some fine paintings that Frances inherited from her uncle, and pillows with fabrics representing trips to other fabulous beach destinations around the world, including Mozambique and Madagascar.

Pine floors and wood-beamed ceilings increase the feeling of this house being part of the rhythm of the world around it. The inside of the home is spare, and that is purposeful. It keeps the focus on the Orzechowskis' outdoor life, which is rich. The family has a close connection to nature, and endeavors to be outside as much as possible. Wotjek and the couple's son surf daily, and encounters with dolphins and even orcas are not uncommon. They tell me that living with as few extras as possible deepens that connection. The name of the house underscores everything they feel about it: They call it Soul Arch, a term that defines a relaxed and stylish stance a surfer assumes when riding a wave. It represents their commitment to a beautiful and balanced life, lived close to nature.

Although there are many routes to happiness, a whole host of which can be achieved through houses near the shore, not every path is the right fit for every person. We instinctively follow our own course. For one family, bright color may rule; for another, it will be a sense of history or togetherness. The quiet, pared-down style exhibited in this house is perfect for this particular family. "This is such a happy place for us. It helps us keep our priorities right," Frances tells me. "This fits our personality so well. Our lifestyle is this house, and this house is our lifestyle."

I admire and appreciate the charm and fantasy of being in a calm space that delivers only what you need—and no more. There is something so restful about that. I also find it to be extremely respectful of the gift we are given when we are near the ocean: Perhaps it really is all we need, and the less we put in our beach homes, the greater the chance that we can see all these things more clearly.

PREVIOUS PAGE: I love how open and serene this space is. The deck surrounding the pool blends in quietly and seamlessly with its surroundings. Wood is a beautiful, durable, and natural material for this home. Structurally strong and visually appealing, the floors and walls will last for years to come.

ABOVE: An outdoor life is key to this family's enjoyment of their home. A stack of surfboards sits at the ready, and a climbing wall outside the shower area awaits. Of course, there are also plenty of areas at home for quiet contemplation.

OPPOSITE: The family is incredibly happy with their house because of the balance they now find in their lives. There's time for surfing, swimming, reading, and relaxing.

ABOVE: An oversize plaid pillow is the perfect spot for reading. A wall of shelves holds plenty of good books, but notably no television. This is a home built on the premise that there are more important things in life to enjoy—like time with nature and time to oneself.

OPPOSITE: A custom wooden daybed and leather pouf in the living area invite rest, repose, and intimate conversation. A wood-burning stove provides a little extra warmth when temperatures drop.

ABOVE: The bath reminds me of a Swedish sauna, with its wood-plank floors and walls and spare look. It opens to the outdoors and the view, underscoring the family's desire to get back to basics.

OPPOSITE: In the kitchen, the shelving is open, displaying the simplest necessities. The work area and island open to a dining area that embraces a sense of calm with an unadorned Scandinavian-style bamboo table and matching white leather chairs.

SLOW LIVING
Seagrove Beach, Florida

WHEN LIFE IS HECTIC, FAST-PACED, AND full of noise, it's important to have a special retreat where you can pull back, regroup, and recharge. A beach house that is designed for balance, harmony, and quiet moments is often the best answer to the craziness of the world. Happily, at Curtis Zimmerman and Carrie Englert Zimmerman's house along Highway 30A in Florida, there are soothing neutrals and wide water views of the Emerald Coast that immediately reduce tension—meaning the buzz stops here.

Everyone I spoke with for this book told me that the beach is their escape. I discovered a uniform belief that a house by the shore should be a refuge, a place to remove ourselves from the stresses of daily life. I couldn't agree more. This is where we go to relax and, as much as possible these days, to unplug. The water has always been known to have restorative properties and has long lured people to its shores with the promise that things will be better if only we could stop and take the time to stare out to sea. Objective achieved here. "This house immediately calms me down," Carrie tells me. "And I am not a calm person!" An Olympic gymnast (and the first American female to receive a perfect 10 on the floor routine), it is obvious that she is a driven soul with a penchant for hard work, full of nonstop energy. I understand that gymnasts need explosive energy and power to succeed, but of course they also need to achieve and maintain perfect balance—and that comes from the core. I believe that this house is Carrie's core, and I can see that it gives her great strength and serenity.

The tranquil retreat begins as soon as your tires crunch onto the crushed-seashell driveway—the sound immediately soothes. You can see the ocean before you even get out of the car. It has been waiting for you. The palm trees sway, and there is a noticeably relaxed feeling in the air. All is right with the world; everything is in harmony. Good architecture and an amazing location can do this! The tops of the palm fronds just reach the upper floors for an ideal line of sight. The outside of the house is white masonry, a durable construction that is strong enough to withstand hurricanes, but puts one in mind of the peaceful, white-washed homes of Mykonos in Greece.

Because the blue water outside is so captivating and alluring, it is important that the house find a way to invite elements of the sea inside. The walls themselves are the answer. They are made of a luminescent Italian plaster, which allows the reflection of the waves and the light from the sun to bounce freely about the house. The movement of water is mimicked there, as the light strikes the surface and then plays across the walls. Smooth stone and concrete make this home feel a little like a Grecian temple for Poseidon, or a luxury spa. The light is extremely important to the Zen qualities in this house, and the architecture takes maximum advantage of its surroundings. There are huge windows everywhere and few window treatments. The house appears open to the world around it, ready to receive light, air, and all manner of positive vibrations. There is nothing here that closes you off from the environment.

The architectural goal is to have as little as possible between you and the water. There are few obstructions to the view, not an insignificant detail when it comes to this particular tableau. The railings along the porches on the second and third stories are formed by glass panels to ensure a clear vista.

OPPOSITE: The view from the roof is unparalleled; everything is designed to keep your focus on the blue beyond. The railings are see-through, and the pergola and supporting columns are simple and unobtrusive. The white, wave-like sculptural piece doubles as an extra-wide lounger. A built-in sofa and matching large planters channel a Grecian energy.

Accessories and possessions are kept to a minimum— a single piece of white coral on a side table, an unadorned wood coffee table, a fireplace mantel with nothing on it— because, as lovely as they may be, lots of little extras can also be distracting. "The house really is a blank slate," Carrie tells me. With nothing to challenge you, your mind can roam where it likes, not where it is forced to. Pared-down elements reduce the impact of the frenetic world around us. Visitors here don't have to spend time processing things or absorbing new ideas. Instead the brain rests, and the body relaxes, pausing to reflect rather than react.

Being understated and uncluttered has its own rewards, and the Zimmermans are smart not to upset the balance. Someone once told me that it's like taking a bottle of sand and water that has been shaken and then allowing it to settle. The sand eventually sinks to the bottom, and the water remains on the top. Only then can things become clear. "There is nothing contrived here," Carrie tells me. "There is no discussion other than what is happening inside you and what you can see outside." This is a beautiful place to be.

As part of the gestalt, there are no clocks in any of the rooms and no references to time anywhere. Instead, the Zimmermans ring a large bell when they want everyone to come in for dinner. I think this is genius, and it reminds me of the Buddhist bells that are used to put you in the proper mood for meditation and reflection. (There is no yelling or hurrying in a truly Zen household!) Still, with a big business to run—Carrie has been leading an integrated marketing company in Tallahassee with her husband since 1987— and three children to care for, she rarely rests, and she tells me that she sleeps very few hours a night. So for her, slowing down has been a bit of a learning curve. "This is a valuable lesson for me to learn," she tells me. And it can only be taught by living in a quietly relaxed beach house.

PREVIOUS PAGE: The living room doors open to reveal a decidedly balanced composition, with the rectangular pool framed just outside. Everything lines up neatly, presenting the idea of an orderly life. The doors become invisible, giving the house an open-air feel. Nothing prevents you from enjoying what is outside even while you are inside.

OPPOSITE: The simplicity of the design is carried through the furnishings and fabrics, most of which are white or neutral in tone. Instead of using a sofa with a back that would have blocked the view, an upholstered bench does the job here using much cleaner lines.

ABOVE: The staircase is striking and dramatic, with curved ceilings and archways. The black iron light fixture from Paul Ferrante welcomes guests and is reminiscent of a spiral seashell, beautiful in its simplicity.

OPPOSITE: The eat-in kitchen is farmhouse fresh and neatly symmetrical. "I have to stop myself from adding stuff to the house," Carrie admits. It takes a certain discipline for people to live an uncluttered life.

ABOVE: Water views are always restorative. "Guests tell me that they appreciate the restfulness most of all," says Carrie. "It allows their imaginations to run free, and often they find themselves reminiscing about their childhoods." Really, it sounds better than therapy!

OPPOSITE: The master bedroom is a quiet retreat. The truth is you don't need a lot at the beach. The warm, white oak wood floors are durable and well matched to a beach house lifestyle. Natural fibers such as muslins, cottons, and linens are used throughout.

COLOR

Close your eyes and imagine a beautiful beach: turquoise seas, white sand, brown driftwood, blue skies, green palm fronds, a yellow umbrella, an orange buoy, a red sailboat. Our experiences with the coast are almost always tied to color. In our beach homes, it's a joy to bring that sense of sea and sky inside. The right shades, used the right way, can make us feel more cheerful, energetic, and refreshed.

Our brains respond to color in ways that immediately impact our physical and mental states. We have all felt the effects. Red is a dynamic, vibrant color that revs us up. Blue—the color of the ocean—soothes and calms us. Yellow is expansive and sunny, sending friendly vibes our way. Orange is vital and powerful. Violet can feel mystical and spiritual. Black is strong and confident. Gray plays a more subdued role. Brown is earthy, and green is as cool as a breeze.

I am happy to report that bright colors often rule the day at the beach. This is where we have fun. A yellow rug? A bright red garden stool? A pink bedroom? Yes, yes, and yes. Beach houses are ideal places to let the whole rainbow of happiness shine. The homes in this chapter get their energy from knockout colors that light up the lives of the families who live there. A lake house introduces a new color in every room. A Nantucket cottage explodes with hot reds and passionate purples. And a home in Rhode Island fearlessly blends turquoise and coral. I can't resist these cheerful places. Enter any one of these doors and you enter a world without fear, full of shades that promote pure happiness.

RAINBOW CONNECTION
Walloon Lake, Michigan

RED HOUSES ALWAYS GET MY ATTENTION— and I mean that in a good way, because this color is a standout. Red is strong, vibrant, and full of the energy and life you expect to find near the shore. This warm and wonderful cottage on Walloon Lake in Michigan reflects the kind of vitality a house can exude when it is dressed in the right shades. The paint color was custom matched to a vintage paint chip from the original siding—the house was red when the family bought it back in 1989, and it has stayed red ever since, even through a recent renovation guided by interior designer Kathryn Chaplow.

Inside the house, the colors are equally exuberant; the rooms are bursting with greens, yellows, blues, pinks, and purples. How did this little lakeside cottage get such a loving dose of color? The Borisch family started out certain about one thing: They wanted to brighten up their dark cottage. Northern Michigan can get awfully gray about six months out of the year, and in areas like this it is especially important to counteract that with lots of brilliant shades. Now, even when the weather is bad outside, the sun is shining inside.

The decor of the house is heavily influenced by interior designer Carleton Varney's decor for the Grand Hotel on Mackinac Island. Varney is the president/owner of Dorothy Draper & Company, Inc., the first interior design business, started in 1923. Draper was known for her splashy colors and modern baroque style. She fearlessly combined floral chintzes and stripes, checkered floors, and elaborate moldings. Varney's work at The Grand followed suit, with bright colors and robust fabrics, all mixed in eye-catching ways. Being huge fans of the hotel helped Jonathan and

Mary Kay Borisch to make bolder, somewhat riskier choices in their own home. When homeowners tell me that they did something risky in their home, I know that the word fun will follow soon after. Sure enough, as Mary Kay walks me through the colorful plans behind her home's decor, she talks a lot about the good times she has in it. "Our friends are here, and our grandkids are over every day," she tells me.

If you are lucky enough to be invited, you will find that all the furniture is cozy and plush, just right for reading and napping. "It is a happy place," Chaplow says succinctly. She chose a bright yellow for the walls to underscore the sunny nature of the living room—and the family. "Yellow is a really good neutral and, when you look out at the view, compatible with the red porch, the blue water, and the green trees."

In the same room, a dark green velvet sofa with white powder-coated nailhead trim is a focal point. Its traditional, tufted style mixes easily with the light-blue floral chintz fabric on the two super comfortable armchairs that sit opposite. The back pillows have a fringed welt that is delightfully cheeky when thrown on such a serious, English country chair. A classic Chippendale table nearby gets a similar kick with a coat of white paint. On top of it sits a turquoise lamp, a surprise addition to the mix. The yellow shag rug and bright white Jonathan Adler lacquered coffee table provide a colorful counterpoint to everything else in the room.

Chaplow throws the conservative idea of "there is such a thing as too much" right out on its ear. How does it all mesh for one big, happy look? "You just have to keep going with it," Chaplow tells me. She points to the pottery on the mantelpiece that includes almost all the colors found in the room: pinks, yellows, greens, blues—a neat tie-in, especially when set against the white hearth and ceiling.

ABOVE: Beach houses are all about the occupants and the good times they share. Stones etched with the names of family members provide a warm welcome home at the base of the front door.

OPPOSITE: A chandelier in a saturated watermelon red hangs above the white dining room table, quietly but strikingly colorful. On the chairs, a traditional trellis pattern is made more modern in hot pink with a double welting on a moss green frame.

NEXT PAGE: A pink stovetop and oven bring to mind the playhouses and Easy-Bake Ovens of our childhoods. On the countertop and in the glass-front cabinets, yellow and turquoise dishware adds to the fun and ensures that the same mix of bubbly, happy colors is carried throughout the house.

The pottery is part of the homeowners' collection and represents years of memories on the lake.

Upstairs, a hipped roof means lots of sharp angles in the bedrooms, where the ceilings appear to be a continuation of the walls. For this reason, Chaplow decided to paint both the ceilings and the walls the same color. The overall effect is like a playhouse or a jewel box. While lavender is not a classic choice for a master bedroom, it is a clear winner here. In a house that eschews drabness, this is just one more moment where the joy of color shines through. "I really like it. It is very peaceful. But not boring at all," says Jonathan. Boring is something this house successfully squelches at every turn.

Having so many different colors in one house means there is always going to be something interesting to look at. Take, for example, the traditional Chippendale pieces that are painted different colors throughout the cottage. Or check out the dining room chairs in the eating nook, with their pretty diamond trellis pattern. The kitchen shelves are painted pale pink, visible through glass cabinet doors, to match the pastel refrigerator. Chaplow describes the kitchen as having "a vintage, ice-cream parlor look," and I think it looks delicious! "You get swept away from everyday life here," she tells me.

Outside on the porch, life really gets good. This is the heart and soul of the house, and it is where everyone hangs out all day and dines at night. The oversize wraparound porch is a hugely important place for this family. Black-and-white striped fabric on white wicker furniture is a page taken straight from the Dorothy Draper playbook. "I let the red of the house be the star of the show," Chaplow tells me. It was a good decision, crisply set off by the blue waters of the expansive, serene lake beyond.

The good news here is that magic can be made, and that this magic often comes from bold color choices. I love the fact that the Borisch family let themselves be swept away by their colorful dream. With so many children and grandchildren visiting, they knew that they were building memories that would last forever. "This is where you don't have to worry about the rest of the world," Jonathan tells me. Their home is exactly what they want: a comfortable, happy cocoon, but one that's not at all shy about showing its true colors.

ABOVE: Happy hour is made doubly so thanks to gorgeous crystal barware and glass swizzle sticks. Red-and-white polka dot cocktail napkins remind us not to take life too seriously.

OPPOSITE: A sunny yellow living room with a tufted green velvet sofa and floral chintz chairs channels Dorothy Draper. But when I consider the hot pink velvet bench with contrasting green-and-white tape detail on top, I get the idea that this family just wants to have fun. Good for them!

ABOVE: With such a vivid red on the exterior, it makes sense to paint the porch ceiling white and leave the warm Douglas fir floors a natural sand color. The contrast adds drama and beauty.

OPPOSITE: Walloon Lake has long been a draw for summer vacationers. Wonderful homes and cottages have sprung up all along its shores. The area is known for its great boating and fishing, so it should come as no surprise that Ernest Hemingway spent childhood summers here.

FREEWHEELING FUN
Nantucket, Massachusetts

THINK OF HOMEOWNER POPPI MASSEY AS THE Willy Wonka of color. Sky blue refrigerators and purple sofas? Surely this is the type of dream a child with a box of crayons and a good imagination might create. But these can also be inspired, uplifting, and sophisticated choices. Being around so many colors automatically makes me feel like I am carrying a lighter load. The instant mood elevation is thanks to the energy that comes from vivid shades. Massey's little house on Nantucket displays a passionate love for all that is bold and bright. There's nothing better in a coastal home! "I'm a very visual person," she tells me. "The crazy, wild colors I use in this house pump me up. It's hard to stay bummed out here." If colors can do that for a person, I say bring it on.

Massey's palette—which ranges from rich reds and deep purples to lime greens and sunny yellows—stretches the imagination because she finds such creative ways to combine them. With so many beautiful shades and patterns and fabrics, she asks me, why not just try to use them all? I can't think of an answer. And so three different fabrics on one sofa are more the rule in this house than the exception. In the living room, for example, a deep-purple seat cushion with green welting is paired with a back cushion covered in a pink herringbone print. The mix is absolutely delightful.

Before making her final color choices, Massey found it helpful to put all of her fabric samples on a long dining room table so that she could assess them. I think this is a great idea, a good way to avoid making decorating mistakes. Walking by your choices day after day allows you time to decide if you really want to live with that look or not.

Swatches that don't pass the test of time can be removed from the table while the others stay in the race. In the case of this house, of course, there were a lot of winners.

The freewheeling color extends to the kitchen, where appliances (including two ovens) exhibit both brains and beauty. A Turbo Chef oven and Big Chill refrigerator each has a distinctly 1950s look that evokes warm, nostalgic feelings. The metal cabinetry from St. Charles of New York is a colorful throwback to simpler times. When Massey found out that the company made the cabinets in bright red stainless, she was hooked. "That's my favorite color!" she says. But even cooler than that was to pair the red with white walls and stainless steel–rimmed Formica countertops. This combo really puts visual snap into the kitchen.

The walls and floors are all painted white. With a super shiny finish, the effect is not really neutral at all. It's very bright! The open-stud walls, beamed ceilings, and wood shiplap sheeting, which runs horizontally throughout the house, add to the cozy cottage feel. To leave walls open this way, the structure must be insulated from the outside instead of the inside. The finishing touches on the exterior— rakes and fascias, porches and decks, weathered shingles, cottage corners, and exposed rafter tails—maintain a historic Nantucket style and make the house feel like it has always been on the island. No one would know from viewing the traditional and unassuming exterior that the interior is so full of excitement!

Pinks and purples dominate the living room but find their way upstairs, too. Why leave all the happy vibes downstairs? In the master bedroom, white wicker furniture and turquoise

OPPOSITE: Beach houses are the perfect places for children's artwork. Bright, happy, and guileless, the drawings turn this breakfast nook into a cheerful, lively space full of personality. The yellow, vinyl-covered chairs and retro table add to the fun.

elements punctuate the mix. The turquoise coffee table is perfect for displaying a collection of seashells, and the fabric on the cheerful pillows has a coastal wave pattern. Each item speaks to how close this house is to the water. This is a constant thread I see in houses by the sea. Happiness comes from echoing the colors of the beach, so that even when we cannot actually be there, we still are surrounded by its colors.

In the newly created bedrooms in the basement area, there is a surprising lightness of being. Architect Stephen Theroux turned the challenge of renovating the dark basement into an opportunity. "Basement spaces don't have to be nasty," he tells me. By digging to create a walkout area off the sitting room, he allowed light and air to stream in, and changed the whole notion of a basement. A gridded Mondrian-style staircase connects the space with the floor above. Its vertical and horizontal lines neatly offset the more fluid Noguchi coffee table, with its wooden base and curved glass top—a classic piece of modernist furniture from a line originally produced in the 1940s. The midcentury club chairs in the downstairs sitting room are upholstered in orange-and-red Ultrasuede with white welting, livening up the space even more—if that's possible! Not one to leave a blank space alone, Massey printed photos on the vinyl window shades, so that when you pull them down, you are met with a surprise: a fun snapshot. What a great way to take an ordinary element and make it special.

Like many homeowners I spoke with, Massey's version of beach house happy—so dependent on color—suits her perfectly. "I have seen houses done in all different shades of beige, and I suppose that can be restful, but if things are too muted, I just don't enjoy it," Massey tells me. While we all appreciate different looks in other people's homes, it's important to know our own personalities and home decor style. And then, like Massey, run with it. She feels energized every time she comes back to her little place by the sea; it's always a thrill. "I get so excited. I almost can't take it," she says. "I get really happy." For a home to continue to have that effect proves just how powerful color can be.

OPPOSITE: White, open-stud walls provide the backdrop for strong colors, like the deep-purple area rug and lime green chairs. The overriding decorating theme is an Atomic Age look mixed with Palm Springs cool. The colors are what make it all explode like Pop Rocks.

ABOVE: Artwork plays a major role in the kaleidoscope of colors. In particular, a bright piece by Nantucket artist Stephen Pitliuk provides a wonderful note of cheer by focusing the viewer on fun. The work is whimsical and tongue in cheek, and includes many of the colors found elsewhere in the house.

OPPOSITE: The kitchen is a '50s retro dream, with its punchy red metal cabinetry and baby blue Big Chill appliances. A mod pendant light hangs above the sink. Old school signage punches up the all-white walls with cheery sayings such as, "The perks are best here."

ABOVE: In the quiet neighborhood of Siasconset on the shores of Nantucket, traditional gray-shingled houses with romantic white picket gates are typical for the area. Mother Nature is kind enough to add to the party with deep green hedges, tall evergreens, sandy beaches, and an impossibly blue sea.

OPPOSITE: White wicker furniture against an all-white backdrop allows the colorful fabrics to take center stage. The throw pillows have a wave pattern, just right for a beach house. The turquoise plays so nicely with the red that the theme extends to the coffee table. It doubles as a display case for a collection of white shells.

ABOVE: White walls, white window sheers, white bedding, and a distressed white end table are all cottage fresh. But then come the exclamation points of color: a navy blue headboard and an antique turquoise lamp. Its layer-cake shade reminds me of an Etch A Sketch drawing.

OPPOSITE: With friends and family always visiting, bunk rooms are virtually a necessity in houses near the beach. After its renovation, the house now sleeps 20, thanks to rooms like this one! Green duvet covers and pink and purple throw pillows make happy bedfellows.

A BRIGHT SPOT
Wakefield, Rhode Island

THERE IS NO DENYING THAT COLOR HAS A HUGE impact on our moods, and perhaps nowhere is this more evident than in a charming four-bedroom house overlooking Potter Pond in Wakefield, Rhode Island. With its turquoise and orange fabrics and sunny yellow accessories, the house smiles brightly for the camera. From the first time I saw these rooms, I was in love with the bold, vibrant colors—they exude fun and warmth, and are fitting for the young family who lives in this house. There are so many great examples here of how joy can be spread through color.

In the hexagonal, two-story sunroom, a beautiful blue glazed ceramic table takes on different tones as the light shifts in the room. Colors in beach houses can change significantly as the sun moves through the sky and light bounces off the water and grass. For me, this is a big part of the fun of being on the coast. It is a renewable experience, refracting the colors within a house like a prism. The doors to this room can fully retract, turning the sunroom into an outdoor space. If, as in this home, you want to open a room to nature, be sure that your furniture is up to the challenge. Everything here, from the fabrics to the resin coffee table, can live outdoors as easily as it can indoors.

Beach houses almost always include beautiful blues. Boston-based interior designer Rachel Reider explains why she loves using turquoise in particular: "It is a happy, vibrant color that evokes a fun feeling of warm weather," she says. "It reminds us of sea glass and beach pebbles, and is representative of the environment just outside the house." I agree. Turquoise is a perennial favorite of mine. It is a cheerful beach house staple, one that shows up on everything from towels to tunic tops to chairs, and it seems no one can resist its charms.

The owners of this house are no exception. They not only succumbed to the allure of turquoise but embraced it, and they happily let Reider run with it, adding vibrant contrasting colors such as orange and navy that awaken the senses. "Most people get nervous about highly contrasting color palettes," Reider tells me, but this family adored the aliveness of it all. What I find particularly noteworthy about their choice, however, is how safe even these seemingly risky colors can be. Color plays a strong role in the rooms but doesn't overpower them. If you look closely, you can see that at its core, the living room is a neutral canvas, with white walls, a soft gray fireplace, and a beige sofa. Remove the turquoise vase, the orange throw, and some accent pillows and you have a completely different impression. Those who worry that strong color combos are not for them can think about adding them in ways that can be changed out if they tire of the look later. I, for one, am going to take this to heart and try to be braver with my color choices. After all, color equals fun, and we could all have more of that in our lives!

The blue glass wall sconces above the fireplace are a good example of the way that color can punctuate a room with strong points of interest. These unexpected happy notes sing on either side of a painting that anchors the whole room. Lighting can of course do more than just illuminate. It can change your mood, add feeling, focus your attention, or introduce drama. Here, it serves as a reminder that pops of color in strategic places can instantly lift your spirits.

OPPOSITE: The right piece of art can tie everything together, making sense of all the colors in a room. In the brightly hued living room, an abstract painting by Meredith Pardue hanging above the fireplace unifies the wide-ranging color palette of oranges and blues and greens. The room instantly feels more cohesive, and the color choices make perfect sense.

For a young, busy family, bright hues seem obvious, but when creating a happy palette, colors need to be delivered in the correct dose. With four little girls, for example, pink was a natural shade to consider because it offers plenty of girly, frilly fun. But children grow up quickly, and ballerina pink would have worn out its welcome long before the eldest hit double digits. The saturated mulberry tones used in the bedroom are a much more sophisticated and versatile choice. Deep and dramatic, rich but fun, these are rooms that will grow with the girls into the teen years.

The beach is, of course, a naturally happy place where bright colors are right at home. This is a simple truth that cannot be overstated. I think it would be safe to add that people are much less afraid to use dramatic tones in their beach houses. I am guessing that because we are more relaxed at the beach, we are more open to colorful experimentation.

Our love of color may also be linked to the strong emotional attachment we have to our shore homes. This homeowner, for example, says that she is not concerned about resale value because she plans to keep her house forever. "We do whatever we want here because we know we don't ever want to sell it," she says. Owning a beach house is all about heart—and more about passion than reason. I find her take on the subject particularly liberating. If a house is going to be your happy place, revel in what you love—including strong colors—and don't worry too much about what others will think. Things that make you feel good should be treasured.

The result, of course, is that this retreat is a sanctuary. Even with all the effort it can take to get young kids on the road to the beach house every weekend, the house always delivers. "I feel my mood change the minute I walk in. I feel happier, and instantly relaxed, thanks to the cheery brightness within and the views outside," the homeowner tells me. Once here, the family takes long walks around the five acres of land surrounding the house. They have a sailboat, and Dad is teaching the eldest to sail. It is the start of many summers to come, a wonderful medley of colorful memories that the family will cherish for generations.

ABOVE: The ceiling in the sunroom is teak, reminiscent of a boat, and the woodwork is painted white. With a natural, sand-colored porcelain tile floor, colorful textiles, and woven furniture, the overall impression is light and bright, fun and breezy.

OPPOSITE: No beach house is complete without blue glass. Touches of turquoise help the decorating thoughts to remain consistent and compatible. Here, a turquoise vase, delicate bowls, and a seltzer bottle sit atop the dining room table. Adding a navy, green, and turquoise Trina Turk pillow fabric to the mix reminds everyone that they are near the sea.

ABOVE: There's nothing better than a window seat for afternoons at home. This area in the girls' room is painted Beacon Hill Damask by Benjamin Moore, a restful, yellow-green counterpoint to the mulberry colors used elsewhere. The bold window shades and fun pillows give the room its sizzle factor.

OPPOSITE: Deep mulberry tones in the bunk room will be able to grow with the homeowners' young girls into their teen years. Turquoise-and-green bedding from Serena & Lily lightens the look and visually ties it into the rest of the house.

HISTORY

Many houses tell a story. They have been around long enough to earn them that right. And the ideal homeowner is willing to listen. Homes with history are especially common along the coast, where some of our earliest communities developed. As our ancestors stepped off boats and huddled together in seaside villages, the magic and mystery of the beach house began to take hold. Hundreds of years later, we find ourselves still drawn to these areas, and reveling in their ties to the past.

History puts things in perspective. It gives us a sense of time and place, without which we risk losing a sense of our own identity. By protecting the memories of times gone by, we honor our place in the chain of events. Historical items can be beautiful, meaningful, and heartfelt. My beach house is more than 110 years old, and it is exciting to be constantly reminded of what came before us.

The houses in this chapter are all amazing examples of the ways that a connection to history and tradition can increase satisfaction in one's life. A wonderful home on Cape Cod is charming for its rough, unfinished look, an acknowledgment of the fact that it was once a simple fishing lodge. A tiny cottage in Georgia relies on flea market finds and memories to help a woman build a new future. On Martha's Vineyard, wide-plank wood floors and gingerbread trim combine to give the feeling that you have stepped back in time. And in Stone Harbor, New Jersey, one family discovers an honorable nautical history and adds vintage pieces to create a brighter, happier future for a once-neglected property.

AN AUTHENTIC LIFE
Cape Cod, Massachusetts

SOMETIMES WHAT YOU VALUE MOST IS NOT what's ahead of you but what's behind you. I think choosing to live in a house with a past is a way of saying that you treasure tradition and being part of something larger than you are. And that can make you feel grounded. When I spoke with homeowner Kathy Pattison, I discovered that her job has her on the cutting edge of a fast-paced and ever-changing world. (Both she and her husband, Dave Strickler, work for high-tech start-ups.) For them, happiness comes from being able to slow down and return to a simpler time in a rustic beach cottage. And so they chose a decidedly unpretentious house, built in the late 1920s and located on top of a bluff in Nauset Heights, a Cape Cod neighborhood. The houses of that era were basic hunting and fishing lodges, and many were not winterized.

The exposed wood and brick throughout the house were among the architectural touches that most attracted Pattison to it. In its simplicity, I see reduced stress and a slower way of life for its busy owners. She tells me that she feels the same way: "The details in this house have an authenticity that we fell in love with." And so she and her husband set out to make sure that this little two-bedroom cottage would be preserved, despite the fact that they clearly needed to find a way to create a little more space for themselves and their children.

In order to make the house larger, they added a lower level and an extra room. The house now happily can accommodate the many guests that the family hosts. The basement addition made way for a bunk room with six custom beds. The once cramped kitchen was also updated for easier entertaining. Thanks to careful planning, the new areas don't deviate from the look of the older parts of the house. The family's edict: no drywall, only rough, lodge-like pine wood. The pine walls are all painted white for a camp-like feel that matches the home's origins.

To show how serious she was about her devotion to the area's history and tradition, Pattison tells me about a built-in bookcase she had custom made. The woodworker finished it while she was away, and she was dismayed to find it looking so nice when she returned. "It was very polished and finished-looking. I wanted it simple," she tells me, and so she had him remove it and start over. The lived-in look is what she is in love with, and although it sounds funny to purposely avoid perfection, I must applaud her dedication to the charms of the rougher look. The imperfections in the wood ceilings and walls lend the house a comfortable, cozy feel. It's what immediately made me want to include this home in my book. Perfection can feel sterile. Sometimes it's best to embrace a home's foibles rather than correct them. Ask yourself: Is this an actual defect? Or is this a mark of my home's uniqueness?

Where we come from can determine our answer to that question. People who grow up in historic homes often return to that type of house as adults because it makes us feel at ease and happy. This was definitely the case for Pattison, who grew up on a farm that was built in 1791. "The fact that it can last—that this house has always meant something to someone, that it was cherished over the years—that's where the beauty lies," she tells me. "My

OPPOSITE: Pattison says that her favorite area in the house is probably the upstairs loft: "When the sun rises, the upper level is flooded with a gorgeous, warm, orange glow. It makes you want to get up in the morning!" Later in the day, it becomes a quiet reading nook, thanks to comfy cushions and pillows.

grandparents worked the farm before my parents. It's a really special place for me." Now she wants her family to feel the same way about their Cape Cod house. This is a place she hopes will become part of their lives and that one day they will pass on to their children. "It is already a part of who they are," she says. "It's like an anchor for them." They even had a tree house built on the property, where the kids love to play. That feeling of having a special place of one's own is already instilled in them.

Much of the furniture in the beach house came from nearby—some of it left behind by the previous owners, and some from flea markets. "I love finding things and repurposing them," Pattison says. Among the collectibles she always searches for: vintage games. The fun is in the hunt and the acquisitions. "I look for old board games that I can put up on the wall in the playroom in the basement," she tells me. "I love vintage wooden boxes and I use them like shelves or frames on the wall." I think to myself that this is a particularly happy collection, bringing with it all the good feelings and wonder of childhood days in the summer.

The family is also starting its own history here, and they are leaving their own mark. Pattison knew that she wanted a pebble floor in the shower, but instead of going to the store she took her family to the beach. There, they collected the stones themselves and hand-picked the colors they wanted. "I always point the shower out to people when they tour our house. It's natural and real. Plus it's fun. It's something we did together as a family; that's what makes it special," Pattison says. Other things they do together harken back to simpler times, as well: playing board games, cooking meals, and clamming. "Nothing tastes better than fresh clams. I make a mean chowder," she tells me.

An old house contains things that have been used and reused. It may not be perfect or fancy, but its age and history make it special. You can't help but value and appreciate that authenticity. History keeps this family grounded. History is their anchor.

OPPOSITE: The open-stud walls and wood-clad ceiling lend a charming genuineness to this cottage by the sea. Comfortable furnishings and a large redbrick fireplace feel warm and cozy. There is an organic, laid-back ease to the home's decor.

ABOVE: Old board games grace the wall of the basement-level playroom. The homeowner collects vintage wooden toys and has created a happy grouping that brings back memories of childhood. The blue-and-white striped sofa invites guests to sit and play.

OPPOSITE: Custom wood cabinetry mixes with open shelving. The island and wide-plank wood floors give a farmhouse quality to the kitchen. Although the kitchen is new, it retains a traditional Cape Cod aesthetic and looks like it has been here forever. Antique glass bottles easily add to that old-world charm.

ABOVE: A freestanding white claw-foot tub becomes a natural centerpiece in any bath. Here, it fits the historic feel of the house and reminds one of earlier times. A true luxury item back in the late 19th century, these tubs are always in vogue and similarly speak to the luxury of being able to have a long soak after a day at the beach.

OPPOSITE: Worn floors and custom built-ins give the house an easy, relaxed attitude. In the children's bunk room, rope details set a nautical tone. A set of steps becomes a bookshelf—and a clever place to display all those winning ribbons kids bring home.

ABOVE: This quaint Cape Cod cottage enjoys a prime location, with an expansive view of the Atlantic. The eyebrow roofline and gray shingles exude character. An American flag hanging just outside the front door is a welcoming touch.

OPPOSITE: Nauset Heights is a charming beachfront community on Cape Cod in East Orleans, Massachusetts. Originally inhabited by the Nauset Indians, the area retains its unspoiled, natural charm today. Area residents are deservedly proud of its rich history and beautiful vistas.

THROUGHOUT TIME, **THE SEA AND SKY**
HAVE SOOTHED US, KNITTING US TOGETHER IN A LONG HISTORY OF
LIFE'S BEST MOMENTS

HOMEMADE MEMORIES
Whitemarsh Island, Georgia

RED AND YELLOW STRIPED PILLOWS ARE tossed on a comfy white sofa, a vintage red Coca-Cola sign hangs on a glossy white shiplap wall, and an old fan of indeterminate years sits on an antique side table. History is almost everywhere in Linda Martin's tiny 1930s cottage on Whitemarsh Island, Georgia. From talking with her, I can clearly see that living with history and with happy memories is what keeps her optimism alive.

Martin tells me that she met her husband when she was just 15 years old, and was married by the time she was 17. Most of her memories are tied to him; they had grown up together and built a life as a couple for 40 years. But when he died, she found herself untethered. She left behind everything she cherished and moved several times, always to new condos and places without meaning, memory, or history. "I was running away from myself," she admits to me. "I ran for 12 years, but I finally came home to the island we loved and decided to renovate the old cottage on our property."

It was by all accounts a wise decision. I think it was only by returning to her past that Martin was able to build a future for herself. She contacted her good friend Jane Coslick, a designer and preservationist familiar with the challenges and rewards of old cottages. Together, they set out to build a safe haven for her there. "Jane said, 'I want you to sit on that porch and learn how to be at peace,'" Martin remembers. Retaining the history and traditions of the place helped her achieve that. Now, she tells me, friends, kids, and grandkids all cram into the cozy cottage, filling it with noise and love and happiness.

Coslick talks to me about her role as a preservationist almost as though she were a therapist. She prefers to say positive things about old houses, not negative things. Her advice: Learn to love those old doors and old pine floors. I believe that this attitude toward our architectural and design heritage can have far-reaching effects on our lives and our sense of well-being. "Preservation is all about happiness to me," says Coslick. "It keeps us connected to our past and our future." In this case, focusing on a careful and respectful renovation truly changed Martin's life.

Coslick started by thinking about the light. Martin had bought new windows for the cottage, and had begun to install them, but Coslick talked her into reinstating the originals. "Windows are so important in old houses," Coslick says. "These were wood windows with wood trim, and they were the soul of the cottage. If you lose the windows, you lose everything about the house. You take away its energy."

The spaces needed to be open and inviting, so Coslick took down a wall in the living room in favor of a floor plan that allows you to see straight through from the front door to the back door. Keeping the design open, she tells me, allows thoughts and feelings to flow more easily. Semi-gloss white paint reflects and glows on wood walls, making the most of a small space. Although the house is painted all white, it doesn't look colorless, thanks to bright pops of primary shades throughout. A tomato red on an antique ship's lantern, cheerful yellow on an end table (once a typewriter stand), and serene blues on lamps and accessories make the house feel peppy, not plain.

The wood in the house is original. There is no drywall used anywhere. There is a Dutch door—old, paneled doors

OPPOSITE: "This is not a fancy house. This is a lived-in house," says homeowner Linda Martin, who enjoys surrounding herself with organically collected pieces and well-worn vintage items. The red Coca-Cola sign always brings back good memories. Each piece comes with a story, and in its telling, there is comfort.

ABOVE: A white picket fence and a screened-in back porch are two immediate routes to old-world charm and happy times. They encourage a connection to the outside world and create inviting areas for guests. The red-and-white striped cushions are as cheerful as candy canes at Christmas.

OPPOSITE: The tiny dining area fits a round wood table and a few metal chairs. It feels warm and intimate, thanks in part to the reclaimed wood on the breakfast bar. Pine floors add to the home's historic value. The chandelier above is covered with shells for an eclectic, cottage-by-the-sea look.

give a sense of comfort. Hollow doors tend to feel, well, hollow. Any leftover wood scraps were lovingly recycled into the kitchen island. They came from bedrooms that had been painted colors like Pepto Bismol pink and spearmint green in past years. They have been sanded down a bit, but not so much that you can't still see a hint of their original colors. The result reminds me of a cheerful collection of pastel Popsicle sticks.

The place is chock-full of old things, each one attached to a memory. An oil lamp that once belonged to Martin's great-grandfather occupies a corner of the living room. She also has her grandfather's schoolbooks, a bench made of old wood in the sitting room, and a cabinet that belonged to her parents. "I love it because the house is *me*. Everything here represents a part of my life," she says. This is exactly what you want to be able to say about a home.

Even though the small house is full of treasures, I am surprised to notice that it does not feel crowded or like a dusty, overstuffed museum. One way to accomplish this is to keep your belongings pared down to the essentials. If, like Martin, you have a lot of things to display, consider storing some items for a while, and then rotating them into the mix later—they'll feel like new. Trying to showcase everything you own all at the same time can be overwhelming. I recently rearranged a bookcase full of vintage finds and discovered that just by taking a few things away and moving other items around, the whole room looked fresh again. Less turned out to be more. It helps that in Martin's home, things are kept simple. "I advised her to hang one painting and one vintage sign, and then place a few starfish on a windowsill," Coslick says. "It's not complicated, but it's not boring either."

The only new things Coslick added to the house were a white picket fence and a swing—both, I would say, elements of a happy life. They allow Martin to be outside, where she can hear the birds and feel the breeze. "It has been a long journey," Martin says. But she is home at last, swinging on her front yard swing or relaxing out back on her screened-in porch. She has achieved peace, love, and happiness, all in 670 square feet.

OPPOSITE: The screened porch is a much-loved part of the house. The classic red-and-white striped fabric with navy blue piping is crisp and cheerful. The red shutters with their whimsical cutouts are from the Jane Coslick Cottage Collection.

ABOVE: A vintage yellow typewriter table has been rethought as an end table, and a red lantern originally belonging to the homeowner's great grandfather now provides a decorative touch in the all-white room. The colorful oyster shell painting, by local artist Bellamy Murphy, adds a modern element. Mixing old and new makes things more interesting.

OPPOSITE: The bedroom is a place for gentle repose and quiet thoughts. V-groove paneling on the walls and ceiling is painted white. Sparsely decorated, the bed is the focal point. Frilly white linens are both chic and girly. A folksy tablecloth from Anthropologie is used as a bedspread.

HISTORY REPEATING
Stone Harbor, New Jersey

I HAVE A PARTICULAR AFFINITY FOR OLD HOUSES, perhaps because I grew up in one. They make me feel safe and warm, and remind me that the concept of beach house happy is something that can be passed down from generation to generation. I was drawn to this adorable cottage on the water in Stone Harbor, New Jersey, because its recent renovation managed to turn back the clock and show real respect for its roots. The result exudes happiness.

The cottage dates to 1942 and it has plenty of stories to tell. The trick is to let those stories bubble to the surface through the right choice of architectural improvements, paint colors, home furnishings, and even artwork. Over the years the house had suffered a series of questionable renovations that led the homeowners to wonder if it should be torn down. The worst was perhaps the dropped ceilings, which imprisoned the house in a 1970s funk. It's not uncommon for old houses to end up with a scary mishmash of styles, layered over time. But the good news is that they can usually be brought back to life, often just by being faithful to the homes' original history.

That job was given to designer Michael Murphy. When he started telling me about the renovations, I was swept up in his contagious enthusiasm for the nautical history and vintage finds that informed its decor. At first, he only saw signs of neglect and poor judgment. But when he scratched away at the surface he found that the house held secrets to a past that indicated a brighter, happier future. There were hardwood floors beneath the carpeting. Behind the drywall he found beadboard on the walls. Plus, he discovered beamed ceilings! The more he stripped away, the more he became convinced that this little seaside cottage

could be rescued. "I felt like a pirate digging up treasure!" he tells me. He soon convinced the owners to let him restore the house rather than raze it.

I applaud his tenacity. Like me, Murphy is influenced by his own past. I think his desire to maintain the integrity of the home and honor the history of the area was personal as much as it was professional. He told me that he spent summers on the Jersey Shore as a child, back when small beach houses were the norm and long before communities like Stone Harbor became increasingly populated with extravagant homes. "I wanted to research the history of this house and bring it back to its original layout and life," he says. As someone who owns an early-1900s house, I can relate to the hunt for information about its past. I, too, have scoured old photos looking for hints and wondered about what came before. Did the porch have an awning? What color was the ceiling painted? It can be very gratifying to find architectural elements or even colors that are original to the period and therefore feel the most authentic.

Often the answers are right there in front of you. Murphy began by searching the house itself for clues about its former life, which is how he uncovered a sign left behind by the United States Coast Guard. It seems that the military had used the home's dock to help with the war effort during the 1940s. A carpenter was able to turn that white sign, with its blue block letters, into a tray that now sits on a large ottoman in the living room. Something like this might easily have been thrown away. Instead, it became a focal point for the designer and a pivotal moment in the renovation of the house.

I believe that good decorating often starts with a single object like this. From there you can build outward, adding layers to the main idea. Before you throw something away,

OPPOSITE: The house, named Miss Conduct (also the name of the family's beautifully restored Chris-Craft boat), was built in 1942 and has a proud history as a Jersey Shore summer cottage. Now painted a custom blue with white railings, it is a cheery reminder of a simpler time. It is filled with flea market finds, such as the eagle on the gable above the front door.

MISS CONDUCT

10729

think about whether it can be recycled. For example, I still have some wooden shutters that were at one time removed from my Victorian-era home. They make a great statement now hung on a wall. We also found an old door in our basement that we were able to refinish and install when we added a new entrance to the house. By strengthening the historical roots of the house, you add more good feelings to your happiness bucket.

This is exactly what Murphy set out to do, as he began collecting vintage finds from the 1940s and '50s. His quest took him to flea markets and vintage shops from Provincetown, Massachusetts, to Williamsburg, Brooklyn, and from Maine to Maryland. The pieces he found not only suited the house, but also the family that would live and play here. With five children and an active roster of summer activities, fancy untouchables would have curtailed family fun. The house needed to be low maintenance and comfortable (my own beach house ethos, as well). Murphy's flea market finds were decidedly not precious, allowing everyone to breathe easy and live the kind of life that the Jersey Shore promises: relaxed, restorative, simple.

If your house begs for the same, consider combing nearby estate sales and flea markets on weekends. Murphy told me he was often surprised to discover pieces that he originally thought might have gone for $2,000 selling for only $20. "I began to make a game of it. Could I keep all my finds under $50?" Most were.

The historical thread Murphy followed led easily to a home that radiates warmth. For me, this is where the feel-good nature of the house is centered: in everything from the large vintage American flag hanging from the staircase to the tiny decorative sea horse element on a bedroom wall to the colorful, weathered buoys hanging on the outside of the

house and the historic blue paint on the exterior. "By using these items, you are saying there was someone here before you. And you want it to continue on after you," he tells me.

There is a sense of pride in being able to preserve history, and it connects you to the past in a very positive way. "You have put yourself in the timeline," Murphy says. As an added benefit, a house with history is unique, never cookie-cutter. When a house is this comfortable with its past, it makes us comfortable, too. You just want to hang out there. That, after all, is what a beach house is all about. And those who do decide to stay are well cared for here. The owners are happy to accommodate a crowd: The house now sleeps 16. For example, in one room, multiple bunk beds hang from the ceiling.

I find that one of the most remarkable things about this happy house is how history has managed to repeat itself. The house has a twin, an identical cottage right next door, also built in the '40s. The two structures were built by a father for his two daughters, and there the sisters lived happily side by side. Now, almost 75 years later, the current homeowner's sister has bought the house next door and restored the twin dwelling to its full potential, as well. The cottages remain side by side—one painted red and the other blue, with a sister in each—the result of a happy history repeated, and the promise of a happy future.

ABOVE: The sea horse is one of those magical flea market finds that can always be used somewhere in a beach house. Honoring a home's history with vintage pieces creates conversation and adds meaning. The items are unique. No one can say, "I know exactly where you got that," or "I have the same thing."

OPPOSITE: Nautical is nice with an enormous vintage flag and wooden ship model. The rope railing was made from old Air Force parachuting lines. The beadboard walls and sculptural ceiling beams were uncovered during the renovation and brought back to life.

ABOVE: An old sewing machine table from a Brooklyn factory warehouse became the dining room table. You can still see where the machines were once screwed into the wood. Now mounted on hairpin legs, the table can drop down from 36 inches to 18 inches as needed.

OPPOSITE: The kitchen remains open to the rest of the house, making it easy access for all. The stools at the bar were salvaged from an old diner in Brooklyn. Wonderful whimsical touches abound, from a ship's wheel that holds wine bottles to a decorative rooster plate.

ABOVE: Extra beds are always in demand at a beach house, especially when there are lots of children. A rosy geometric print on the quilts and sheer window shades make this guest room bright. A lighthouse replica sits on the nightstand, another one of the carefully curated nautical touches that appears throughout the house.

OPPOSITE: Murphy designed the bunks after beds on military ships. The hanging system is also modeled after those on boats, a practical solution to the threat of water coming in and flooding the floor. That's one of the great things about looking to history for decorative ideas: Often they are extremely pragmatic concepts.

ROMANCING THE PAST
Martha's Vineyard, Massachusetts

THOSE LUCKY ENOUGH TO MOVE TO MARTHA'S Vineyard always say they never want to leave. Now that she owns a summer home here, interior designer Tracey Overbeck Stead knows the feeling—and she plans for her house to be passed down for generations to come. She tells me that one of her neighbors has managed to keep his house in the same family since it was first built. "This is a magical place," she says.

The Vineyard—with a history of European settlers dating to the 1600s—teems with stories, many of them told through the island's architecture. In the community of Oak Bluffs, the fanciful Victorian cottages are fearlessly painted stunning shades of ballerina pink, cornflower blue, mint green, and sunny yellow, as cute as a box of assorted Peeps at Easter. About 300 gingerbread cottages built in the 1860s sit snugly packed together, an amazingly well preserved collection of Gothic-style Victorian architecture. The Steads' cottage is one of my all-time favorites because it has such a warm, genuine feel.

Oak Bluffs is a step back into another century, with mostly pedestrian streets and the freedom that comes with Mayberry-style values. Things seem simpler here; neighbors help neighbors. While children ride on scooters and play Wiffle Ball in the street, grown-ups gather with homemade cookies and summer salads. There are puppet shows, movie screenings, and talent nights.

The community's fierce respect for its past is a big part of the draw for new residents like Tracey. She recalls going into a neighbor's house and seeing a vintage baby carriage sitting on the stairwell. Then she saw a photo from the 1800s with that same baby carriage in it, in use!

"It gives me so much joy to see that," she tells me. The Camp Meeting Association neighborhood offers her a strong sense of place. When choosing a summer home, she tells me, "We chose old-school. There is a rich history here for our children to experience."

It's also why Tracey and her husband, Ethan, have done little to change their cottage and have made every effort to restore it to its original glory. Inside this tiny gem are wide-plank pine floors, gingerbread trim, and lots of antique whaling memorabilia, including flensing tools and scrimshaw. These houses were built without pretension in an era of practicality—Tracey tells me that old tree stumps act as a foundation and hold up the house. They didn't change anything architecturally except the bath. "The only thing we did was to take the paint off the pine floors and bring them back to the original wood," she says. Her Gothic windows have original rose glass. "One of the panes is cracked but I absolutely refuse to replace it."

This makes me laugh, but I completely understand the sentiment. Certain things are irreplaceable, and it is often better to live with some imperfections than to live without the authenticity that historical details deliver. I can relate, too, because I have a 100-year-old doorknob on my front door that none except those with "the knack" can turn. I would never replace it even though it can sometimes take me several tries to open or close it.

I was pleased to see that Tracey chose paint colors for the inside of her home that are as soft and subtle as an oft-washed T-shirt: Rainsong by Pittsburgh Paints, a pretty greenish blue, graces the sitting room, and pale pink is on the walls of the master bedroom. Everywhere I see proof

OPPOSITE: Because the original houses of the era were built fairly inexpensively, they have plain, wide-plank pine floors and pine walls. I love the rustic charm of the place. It reminds you what real beach houses are all about. Older pieces, such as the white antique ship's wheel used here as a chandelier, are recycled and given new life.

ABOVE: The front porch is an important part of life here. Other families come out on their porches, too, and the kids play together. It is nice to see history repeat itself in a neighborhood that has been a tight-knit community for generations. The parents and grandparents also played together as children.

OPPOSITE: In the kitchen, glass-front cabinets add to the ease and transparency of the house. Seeing through to the all-white tableware is at once practical and soothing. The dishwasher is a slim 18 inches wide, helping provide modern comfort efficiently. The vintage-style refrigerator is a soft blue, so the kitchen feels light and airy.

that quiet tones can come from colors besides just white. The slipper chairs are covered with a blue-and-tan striped fabric. The brown rattan sofa feels relaxed and cozy, quietly blending in with everything around it. Tracey has many pieces of furniture given to her by relatives in Texas, allowing her personal history to mix with the history of the island. I love that nothing in this house shouts, "Look at me!" It all whispers, "Live with me."

For the exterior of the cottage, she introduced a sea green-and-turquoise palette, adding orange accents in neat stripes to the balustrades. Naturally, all of her color choices were approved by the neighborhood association so that they would be in harmony with the other homes. Here, each cottage has a name. The Steads call theirs The Whale House. Of course, I must know the story. "I have an obsession with whales," Tracey tells me. "When we bought this house my son was very young, but he noticed a whale cutout near the front door and suggested calling it The Whale House. The name stuck. Now I collect all kinds of whaling antiques. I purchase them at flea markets on the Vineyard, so a lot of it is local."

Traditions like these are a way of life in this tight-knit neighborhood, where people return year after year to celebrate Grand Illumination in August, when every house hangs Japanese paper lanterns. When I ask, Tracey tells me that her family has created their own traditions, as well. "We've taught our kids that you go to the beach every day, no matter what the weather. It never gets old. It's always beautiful, even if it's raining. We eat dinner on the beach at least three times a week. We live in a bubble."

But they have everything they need in this 900-square-foot, three-bedroom cottage. The lack of space, she tells me—doing without all the objects and accessories that tend to fill up bigger houses—is liberating. "After a week on the island, our cottage almost starts feeling too big to me. You find that you don't need any more stuff." What she does have is less than perfect, and that suits her just fine. "We drive a beat-up Land Rover that can only go about 35 miles an hour, but that's OK—that's the speed limit here anyway," she says. It's clear that in this community, everyone is very happy to live in the past and let the rest of the world pass them by ... at least for the summer.

ABOVE: The homeowners collect whaling memorabilia, and even named their house The Whale House. Scrimshaw pieces made from whale bones and teeth are on display here, along with natural elements such as shells, stones, and pinecones.

OPPOSITE: Flensing tools and antique harpoons line the walls in the living area. The sofa is made of eco-friendly natural materials. Throughout the house, hemp, linen, and organic cottons are the materials of choice. Rustic browns, terra-cottas, sage greens, and creams rule the day.

ABOVE: The Steads make a point of taking their children to the beach every day. Despite an outdoor shower, sand always manages to find a way into the house. It's a small price to pay, though, and no one really minds. In fact, the middle son, Elliot, prefers things that way. He once told his mother that sand in his sheets helps him sleep better.

OPPOSITE: The bedroom is one of my all-time favorites because it is so romantic. The walls are painted a very soft pink, and white sheers elegantly offer privacy. The Gothic windows still have their original rose glass. The door is painted a soft green. A chandelier from Currey & Co. lends subtle French sophistication to an otherwise low-key space.

SHARING

On the road to personal happiness, nothing seems more likely to speed you along than the feeling that comes from giving and sharing. At the beach, where doors are thrown open, bunk beds await, and large tables are spread with meals to share, it seems easy to enhance this aspect of our lives. In fact, many beach homes are designed for entertaining and socializing, with an eye to accommodating a crowd.

This is where we go to spend quality time with the people who are important to us. By playing games in the backyard or enjoying a clambake on the beach, we are building experiences that will lead to wonderful memories. Stories about annual family reunions, for example—with their midnight swims, clam-eating competitions, or memorable Fourth of July desserts—take on new life as time passes. The pleasure we get from shiny new objects is short-lived, but the joy that comes from our memories of time spent together lasts and lasts.

The houses in this chapter all represent a spirit of generosity. They share some common attributes: relaxed comfort, open spaces, room for guests. A Hawaiian home with a welcoming lanai is the site of many happy family reunions. A shabby-chic cottage in the Florida Keys has a laid-back look that makes guests feel right at home. A Southern California abode blurs the lines between indoors and out, making it more inviting to the neighborhood. And a small house on Lake Michigan has a big heart. When you open your doors, you open the pathway to happiness.

FRIENDS FOREVER

Ludington, Michigan

FROM MEMORIAL DAY TO LABOR DAY, THE cottages in this small town along the shores of Lake Michigan come to life, with doors and windows thrown open to sun and fun. Let the entertaining begin! Happiness stems not only from the bright, light interiors and the white sand and cobalt waters outside, but also from the clans who gather each year to celebrate in a multigenerational mix.

Sharing is the name of the game on the lake: Neighbors exchange gifts ranging from food, drinks, and Popsicles to … painted rocks. Yes, the painted rock is a time-honored tradition here, and it serves as a calling card. Imagine coming home and finding a hand-painted heart, peace sign, or colorful note left there for you, spelled out on a smooth beach rock. This is the type of thing you can treasure forever. But I feel certain that the act of choosing, painting, and delivering the rock to a neighbor engenders even more joy than receiving one. This is because we are hard-wired to feel good about acts of charity and kindness. It is one of the clearly established routes to a greater sense of happiness and well-being for all of us.

Families return year after year, and friendships grow. Bonds form as each new generation arrives—between grandparents, parents, and children. Sociability is practically a requirement when houses are built close together. This is beach living at its best, and it is a signature feature of Dana and Ramsey Small's cheerful home here among 225 similar, turn-of-the century cottages situated around a strikingly beautiful lake. The family's generous spirit is obvious in the home's open floor plan and wonderful, wide porch leading out to the beach. From the kitchen to the living room, there are very few hallways; one room simply unfolds into the next. This allows great flow, not only for light and air, but also for people. There are loads of windows, which, weather permitting, are raised to welcome breezes. "We open ourselves to the outdoors and vice versa," says Dana, who spends time every summer here with her husband and their twins, Matilda and Tate, and the rest of the year in Stuart, Florida, where she owns a popular coastal boutique named Matilda's.

It helps that the house has such a wide porch, which was constructed to feel like an extension of the sandy beach. There is an awning for protection from the sun during the day, and steps running the length of the porch like stadium seating for counting the stars or watching the fireworks at night. Because the house is not terribly large, Dana sometimes pulls the living room furniture outside to create more seating. It transitions to the porch, and the porch furniture moves down to the beach. Genius!

The mood is celebratory—the summer season spans three patriotic holidays (Memorial Day, Independence Day, and Labor Day), and so it makes perfect sense that the house is decorated in reds, whites, and blues. The colors are practically synonymous with coastal style, and they help to amplify the small spaces. At the beach, those close quarters are often the most dearly cherished. They add to the sense of intimacy and increase opportunities for shared memories and special moments. Plus, they reduce the amount of time the family has to spend

OPPOSITE: Patriotic moments abound during the summer season, and the Fourth of July is a favorite holiday for the Smalls. The children take care to fly the flag high as they run along the beach. Of course, red, white, and blue is a classic coastal combination that gets equal play inside the house.

cleaning and maintaining the premises. Less time working means more time for playing by the water!

Inside, photos line the walls. The Smalls love to include shots of friends as well as family. "By putting friends on the wall, we are letting them know how much we love them," Dana tells me. The family's penchant for entertaining and togetherness is now being passed down to their children, who already consider this house their happy place.

Summer nights lend themselves to suppers for crowds ranging in size from four to 40, and a small breakfast nook is the site of an annual Jenga competition, when as many as 14 adults squeeze in to play. I personally find these little spaces so appealing, and the blue-and-white toile fabric with sailboats and buoys on the seats adds to the charm. As more and more friends arrive, "We're practically sitting in one another's laps," Dana says. But that only furthers the sense of camaraderie and togetherness. For the kids, the Smalls host a Connect 4 tournament, played as a round robin. Other parents, they tell me, are shocked to see their perennially "bored" and "plugged-in" children totally focused on the game and happy to set aside their beloved handheld devices. That's what a good beach house experience can do for you. It is so rare to immerse ourselves in those moments, without distractions, which is why Dana tells me she has one rule: "Come to my house and I will feed you and serve you drinks," she says. "But no cell phones. I believe in good old-fashioned family fun."

It's an approach I wholeheartedly support. I highly recommend board games and puzzles as beach house must-haves, ahead of TVs or sophisticated sound systems. After all, you already have a view and the sound of the waves. Keep games in sight and easily accessible and I guarantee you that they will be used. Some of my best nights at the beach have been spent playing games with people whose company brings me joy. So what makes this family happiest? "It's the friends and family that make this place special for us," Dana tells me. Aha. Just as I thought.

OPPOSITE: The painted rock is a time-honored tradition in this lakeside community, and anyone with a paintbrush can get in on the action. The rocks have been known to replace more conventional forms of communication—a phone call, a text message, or even a Hallmark card. Left on doorsteps, they simply say, "I care." I love this idea.

ABOVE and **OPPOSITE:** The walls sport classic beadboard, painted Blue Hydrangea by Benjamin Moore. Hooks are a beach house necessity for everything from hats to towels. The breakfast nook has a locally made butcher block table and cozy banquette seating covered in blue-and-white cotton with a pattern of sailboats and buoys.

NEXT PAGE: The living room chairs are covered with removable slipcovers that can be thrown in the wash. White doesn't fade the way patterns can, so it's actually quite practical at the beach, even if you have young children. The Pottery Barn picnic table bench is the perfect, easy solution for a coffee table in a small space.

ABOVE: Dana and her daughter, Matilda, enjoy some cold refreshments together. Entertaining at the beach is made easy with a simple white wicker bar cart rolled out onto the porch. It contains all the essential summer classics, including iced tea. A blue-and-white striped outdoor rug feels good underfoot.

OPPOSITE: Tate's bedroom does double duty as a playroom. A red wall lends drama and energy to the small space, and a king headboard and twin bed turned sideways fool the eye into imagining a much larger space. Colorful buoys hang from the ceiling trim. Paper lanterns add soft lighting to keep the atmosphere low-key.

OPPOSITE: The emphasis here is on being outside and enjoying the beach and lake. The deck runs the width of the house—just deep enough for a table and chairs—and is where everyone hangs out. A red gingham fabric on white wicker furniture is a classic touch. With a retractable awning for a little sun protection, it is the ideal spot to be. Steps lead down to the sand, where more seating options can be found. A round table and chairs match the deck furniture.

A WARM WELCOME

Maui, Hawaii

THE LANAI IS THE HAWAIIAN VERSION OF A really big welcome mat. Actually, of course, it is a porch—the place where you invite your guests to sit, where you can hang out all day and sometimes even sleep at night. If the wind dies down and you're feeling hot, you can just move to a different part of the lanai for better breezes. The lanai is the center of all activities at Bill and Candace Raboff's home on Maui. Candace is a big fan of her 750-square-foot, wraparound outdoor space, and I can see why. Thanks to the lanai, she has almost doubled the under-roof space for the house. Outside, she can entertain happily for hours, for this is where the house can best be shared. And as anyone with an island house will tell you, sharing is what it's all about. There is no shortage of friends and family who would like an opportunity to enjoy a little bit of Hawaii's tropical paradise with you.

Thanks to the Raboffs' generosity, this is a house that gives to others almost as much as to the homeowners themselves. Candace's eldest sister, for example, stayed here while recovering from hip surgery and believes that the house had a hand in healing her. This is a theory I have heard many times before, and I truly believe in the restorative powers of sand, sea, and salt air. How much joy Candace must have gotten from the thought that she was able to help her sister this way! She has shared the house with all four of her sisters and their families, and loves being able to host everyone. There are three bedrooms and plenty of bunks, so she can accommodate a crowd. There's even a cute little guest cottage next door that can sleep more. "I almost feel guilty being so happy here," she tells me, so she makes sure that plenty of other people get to experience that same joy.

Inside, whitewashed walls and open, airy rafters give the home a camp-like feel. The wide-plank floors are hickory and pecan; the veining in them adds warmth. Because of the brilliant natural ambient light throughout the day and into the late evening, the Raboffs opted only for lamps for reading. There are no closed spaces; everything is connected. All the rooms are positioned for maximum airflow from the trade winds. Set a half mile back from the water, the house gets great breezes, helped along by the large, custom, mahogany French doors that always remain open when they're home. Like all good island houses, this one feels comfortable, not overly formal or fancy. Comfort is what attracts houseguests most.

The interior design is well set up to host a steady stream of family and friends. For help, Candace turned to designer Susan Trowbridge, a close friend from Santa Fe, New Mexico, where the Raboffs have their primary residence. The house feels lived in and relaxed, in part because of its mix of old and new. "Candace would rather find something old than have it made new," Trowbridge tells me. Case in point: a pair of original rattan chairs wrapped in leather. These old McGuire chairs with woven leather from the 1960s were a special vintage find, now prized by the Raboffs. The dining room table is antique mahogany, and the guest room bed was made out of two antique French twin beds. Antiques lend character and create a home that is anything but stuffy. Interestingly, there are no closets. Instead, the family relies on armoires and the idea that you need to keep very little at the beach—a few sarongs, a bathing suit, and some flip-flops. Who needs a closet? By leaving them out, they maximized floor space.

OPPOSITE: The wraparound lanai has ocean views. The flooring is ipe, a particularly warm and resilient wood. Rattan furniture and vintage textiles provide comfy seating for guests. A surfboard is never far away, a tribute to the family's love of water activities.

The home is contemporary in turns, but there is also a French country vibe. And a 19th-century Asian elm table proves that the mix can be even more eclectic and include many periods and styles. The juxtaposition of old furniture with new, and antiques with Pier 1 purchases, allows for a unique look. This is how the home gets an infusion of personality and charm—by not sticking to a preconceived notion of matching furniture sets. That gives a sense of age and legacy, as though the pieces have all been there a long time. Plus, a home like this is easier to share with others because it has a lived-in feel, as opposed to being pretentious or fussy. "People feel inherently at home with our things," Candace tells me.

The kitchen, as in most homes, is a central hub. Open shelves make everything accessible, which is especially important when guests are in residence. No one has to search for items or dig through cabinets to find what they want. The stainless steel island is serviceable, allowing multiple people to be in the kitchen at the same time. "We all cook," Candace says, so they need to be in there together. Everything has its place for ease of use: The pans are right next to the stove. The countertops are marble. The kitchen is constantly busy. "We eat a lot!" says Candace with a laugh. For a family with a very active outdoor life, this makes sense. A typical day might include an early breakfast, followed by a second breakfast to fuel up before surfing or snorkeling, and then a packed cooler for lunch on the beach and a big meal at dinnertime.

But the star of the house is, of course, the location. You can feel the presence of the island life around you everywhere you look, thanks to lush landscaping and water views. Naturally, the outdoors are a big part of the Raboffs' lives—Bill and the two girls love to surf. Just as the ocean provides them with respite from the stresses and obligations of their mainland lives, so too does this house offer everyone who visits a quiet retreat. By sharing their happy place with others, they only increase their good feelings about their home.

OPPOSITE: The open and airy living/dining area feels almost barnlike, with soaring rafters and open-stud walls. There is no air-conditioning—thanks to the trade winds, it is rarely needed. Special hooks (or sometimes just some coconuts) keep the French doors open to the breeze. The furnishings are an eclectic mix of fab finds. The mirror was purchased from a clothing shop! The big, solid, dining table is antique mahogany. The chandelier hanging above it is a whimsical touch.

PREVIOUS PAGE: Even with all the hours they spend in the ocean, there's still always time for a swim in the saltwater pool, which isn't heated and uses a solar-powered pump. The Raboffs are big believers in not having more than what is necessary. They also believe in conserving and being ecological. They collect rainwater at their house and have a 28,000-gallon tank with a filtration system.

ABOVE: Wooden bunk beds with cozy quilts ensure that there is space for all. The wicker rocking chair was a flea market find. **OPPOSITE:** The rose-colored wall in the kitchen is a standout. The drawer faces take it a step further, with turquoise and yellow for a pop of color. A farm table balances the stainless steel stove and island, adding warmth. Old-school drop pendant lights have understated appeal.

SHARE TACTICS

Newport Beach, California

N THIS LIFE, THERE ARE BACKYARD PEOPLE, and there are front yard people. One look at the Lipkowski house in the family-friendly community of Peninsula Point in Newport Beach, California, and I can see that Jim and Tina are definitely front yard people. Front yard devotees want to put themselves out there, greeting the neighborhood full-on and inviting interaction with the community. Backyard lovers prefer the idea of retreating to a private space away from the street, with less noise, less commotion, and more time to oneself. But this family is clearly happiest when surrounded by friends. And so they created a home that encourages neighbors to stop in for a visit. Handmade swings hang from a tree out front for their two daughters to play on, and a fire pit on the patio encourages warm conversation. The area is a safe and easy place for their girls to grow up, a place where they can skateboard and hang out with family and friends, a place that lends itself naturally to convivial gatherings. Above all else, this home was designed to be welcoming.

They hired designers (and sisters) Karen Brown and Kristina Mathiesen to completely transform the house into a home they would be proud to share with others. Brown and Mathiesen tell me they start every project by trying to understand as much as they can about their client's personality. In this case, the designers' goal was to create a home as social and outgoing as the family is. The Lipkowskis' natural magnetism was key, Brown tells me: "They always have smiles on their faces. They are so content in their home and as part of this community."

Ever the gracious hosts, the family thrives most when they are being hospitable to others.

The outside spaces definitely reflect this. "The front yard has become like their backyard," says Brown. "They tend to entertain there more than anywhere else." Because it is a beach community, and the Southern California weather is beautiful year-round, the family is always outside, and the doors remain open. The hope is that neighbors will come up off the sidewalk and drop in on the festivities. To that end, the house encourages a blurred line between indoor and outdoor spaces. Large French doors allow easy access from the living room to the front of the house with its courtyard, fire pit, and dining table. There is a dining table inside and another one outside. More people? They just add more chairs. Everyone can gather around.

Meanwhile, inside the house there are very few walls downstairs, meaning that the whole floor plan is quite open and inviting. The eating area, family room, and outside living room are all connected for easy entertaining. Dated wallpaper was removed during the renovation, and walls were painted white, making the house feel fresh and light. Colorful accessories and art throughout add interest and liveliness, important in a house that hums and buzzes with people and conversation.

The modern kitchen, with its built-in breakfast nook, is also a major social center. The original kitchen had to be completely torn out to create this new family-friendly space. The designers added a big island, which is perfect for hanging out and being together. In my experience, if you love to entertain, the kitchen is going to be the most high-traffic area. Guests will want to be where you are. That's

OPPOSITE: No childhood is complete without the classic rope swing. Hanging these swings from a tree out front means the fun can spill out onto the sidewalk, where curb appeal translates to playground appeal. The swings were custom made by the designers' father especially for the girls, who can play on them while Mom and Dad watch from the front porch.

why it's best if the kitchen is large and open to other rooms. Yes, it may be a little messy, but kitchens like this one exude a warm and wonderful type of controlled chaos: one person using the blender to make a fruit smoothie, someone else reaching into the refrigerator for some leftover pasta, a child sitting on a countertop to talk with the cook, a friend chopping vegetables at the sink. The right kitchen layout can be conducive to these happy scenes. In order to keep the feel timeless, the designers used a neutral palette with simple marble slabs and white subway tiles. It makes the kitchen a very appealing place to be. To balance the white, there are lots of bright fabrics in bold colors on the nearby breakfast nook banquette and on the throw pillows for the living room sofa.

Kids are an essential part of the good times here. I always feel that beach houses that welcome children are particularly happy places because they speak to comfort over formality. There is no "keep off the furniture" mentality. Instead, there is a big sign in the playroom that spells out the word FUN in lighted capital letters. No one can say they weren't warned that this is a place for celebration and laughter. The decor invites everyone to join the party. "All the kids in the neighborhood go there," Brown tells me. There is even a loft area that adds to the excitement. Just past the FUN sign, there's a ladder, and even though I am a full-grown adult, I must confess that I would be determined to climb it. The cozy hideaway was created out of some empty space above the Jack and Jill baths, a smart use of space. It's outfitted with beanbags and books, and is only about 5 feet high at the most in spots—perfect for all those little explorers, secret clubs, and quiet reading. No wonder that it easily attracts the whole neighborhood!

I find that throughout the house there are eye-catching pieces that make the spaces even more fun to share with others. The mod chandelier above the dining table, the peacock blue settee in the master bedroom, the bright pink sheepskin rug in the girls' room—all of these decorative

elements add up to a memorable look that keeps me wanting to come back for more. I am particularly enamored of the very girly daisy chandelier from IKEA that the designers hung in the daughters' room. "It's whimsical and such a fun fixture," says Brown. The intricate shadows it casts create another moment that can be shared with friends. The unexpected gold pouf and gold knobs on the girls' dresser are delightful. Fun house, indeed!

As much as this home plays host to the neighborhood, the beach—only a block away—is the greatest shared element of all. The family goes there often, along with everyone else, to take advantage of everything this seaside neighborhood has to offer. On weekends, they don't even need to drive anywhere. Their home is the center of the action, and the party comes to them. This openhouse, *mi casa es su casa* attitude brings them a lot of joy. I believe that the energy we put out into the world comes back to us. This house, with its open layout, inviting front yard, and playful decor, is designed with that idea in mind: to welcome neighbors and friends in a big way. I am sure that the love this family gives to their community ricochets right back to them.

OPPOSITE: The bright Trina Turk fabric on the banquette is the big draw here, with its swirling colors of blue, turquoise, and green that tie in nicely with similar shades used throughout the house. Drawers underneath the seats provide needed storage space near the kitchen.

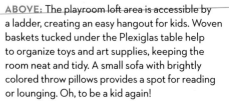

ABOVE: The playroom loft area is accessible by a ladder, creating an easy hangout for kids. Woven baskets tucked under the Plexiglas table help to organize toys and art supplies, keeping the room neat and tidy. A small sofa with brightly colored throw pillows provides a spot for reading or lounging. Oh, to be a kid again!

OPPOSITE: The all-white kitchen is sleek and appealing, with classic subway tiles for the backsplash and a big, marble-topped island. The clean and cool wire counter stools sport citrus seats—a great color choice for a cheerful kitchen. Round white pendant lights are fun and mod. A large, stainless steel refrigerator is big enough to satisfy a crowd of hungry guests.

ABOVE: The designers bravely drew from the groovy '70s for design elements that pack a punch, such as the shag carpet in this bedroom. Rugs can really bring a whole other dimension to a space. You can add color and texture to completely change the look. And shag says that no one is taking themselves too seriously.

OPPOSITE: Even slightly chilly nights don't deter this family from opening the French doors and enjoying their outdoor living spaces. Thanks to a large, square fire pit, everyone can be toasty and warm. Comfy chairs invite you to put your feet up and stay a while. Simple recessed lighting in the overhang keeps the party going after dark.

FAMILY TIES

Casey Key, Florida

WHEN A FAMILY LOVES ITS HOUSE and each other, you can just tell. It shows. Great happiness is certainly evident at Jeff and Nikki LaBelle's bright, busy home on Casey Key, in Florida. I think I know where that happy vibe comes from: It stems directly from the LaBelles' desire to share what they have. They know that they are among the lucky few with a home on an island, the Gulf of Mexico at their front door and an Intracoastal bay out the back. Because they are so uniquely situated for maximum beauty and water views, they feel fortunate to have it all and they want to spread the joy.

"We have people over all the time," Nikki tells me. I can tell that much of her contentment in her house stems from this frequent hosting. I am reminded of a famous saying attributable to Buddha: "Happiness never decreases by being shared." From what I see of beach houses, this kind of happiness can only be multiplied.

With that in mind, the LaBelles have created a home that easily accommodates friends. They bought the house in 2002. It turned out to be a smart tiebreaker for a couple wanting two different things: Jeff, a place on the bay, and Nikki, a place at the beach. Here, they have both and live in harmony! First, they injected the house with some real personality: Sage green paint on the siding and white for the trim gives the house its irresistible Key West character. Then they set about changing every inch of the interiors, renovating to suit their needs and to open up the rooms for the easy entertaining they knew they would want to be doing frequently.

They promptly removed the cold tile floors, replacing them with much warmer, softer wood. When the planks were new, Nikki even encouraged her kids to ride their skateboards across them to give them a distressed look. They also knocked out walls to help the spaces breathe, and raised the sunken family room to join it with the other rooms on the first floor. "It was important to us to make the house feel open," Nikki tells me. "It helps make it feel bigger."

Now, light pours into the whole house through unadorned floor-to-ceiling windows. The living room, dining room, kitchen, and family room are all connected, underlying the LaBelles' love of being together. The furnishings reflect the friendly atmosphere; they include heirloom accents and one-of-a-kind antiques. Nikki has collected pieces from France and from estate sales in the area to give the interiors a laid-back, lived-in look. A white baby grand piano might seem like a formal touch, but it gets plenty of use—two of her children play and take lessons. Everything is clean, fresh, and fun—the perfect reflection of beach house happy.

Nikki favors a shabby-chic style, which is fanciful and pretty but also practical. Guests can feel at home here. The white denim slipcovers are a good example. "They're comfy and baggy," she tells me. "And when I need to, I just throw them in the wash with a little bleach." It's important that everything in the house is easy to care for. In order to be a happy host, you need to be a relaxed host. It's no fun to visit a house where you feel you can't touch anything or sit comfortably anywhere.

The tongue-and-groove walls are all painted white, with touches of pale blue to give the home a true seaside-cottage feel. To add to the storybook look, a single oar painted the same blue hangs on a white wall above a large

OPPOSITE: In the kitchen, the cheerful breakfast nook invites lots of people to squeeze in, thanks to the built-in bench beneath the window. The cabinets are prettily painted the color of the sky on the inside and fronted with glass to display the all-white china. The chandelier is full of sea glass charm.

picture window. And in one bedroom, an antique mirror occupies a prime spot. Made from a salvaged frame, its edges are lovingly chipped and worn, in tune with the soft, white ruffles on the bedding. The windows are hung with simple sheers so as not to obstruct that amazing view of the Gulf. Everywhere in the house, sea glass bottles, seashells, and coral adorn the shelves. It's such a restful and pleasing look, just right for the beach.

Outside, a large teak table helps attract a crowd. And when that doesn't provide enough room, people spill out onto the beach, building bonfires and enjoying the easy connection to the water. The family's lifestyle is outward-looking, a commitment to their love of nature. "Jeff fishes and goes crabbing," Nikki says. "He goes out in the morning and again in the afternoon. The kids paddleboard and surf." The house is set up to accommodate a busy, active crew who spend a lot of time outside. Seven surf-boards hang in the playroom, proving that there's no end to the fun this family has on the water.

With four children and three dogs, the LaBelles are not interested in creating a home that needs constant fuss and attention. That would be exhausting! Instead, they put a good deal of thought into making their home as easy to live in as possible. They get so much joy from that. This is a home so welcoming that people often come for dinner and stay for breakfast. "We like to share what we have with other people," Nikki tells me. "I like having people around. It makes me happy, and it makes my kids happy, too."

The LaBelles have hosted parties with as many as 100 friends at a time, even though their house is not huge—proving that at the beach, it's not the size of your square footage that counts, but the size of your heart. Their gener-osity always pays a big dividend. It's in the smiles and the thank yous they receive from their contented guests. In fact, they find that the more they do for their friends and family, the happier they feel.

OPPOSITE: The living room is a happy, open space with comfy, slipcovered sofas. Coastal touches are everywhere, from the starfish, seashells, and coral on display on tables to the oar used as a handrail on the steps. Distressed wood frames containing pictures of the kids are the only artwork; the wall of photos is a classic beach house look.

THE LABELLES

Jeff, nikki, regan,
noah, xander and bodell

ABOVE: The outside of the house welcomes guests with an inviting white picket fence, an open gate, and glass doors. A hand-painted, tropical sign hanging from the arbor announces that the LaBelles are in residence. Lantern sconces flanking the French doors are a nautical touch fitting for a house right on the ocean.

OPPOSITE: Nothing says "beach house chic" like a quiet blend of aqua, bright turquoise, and soft white. The family loves living near the water and have incorporated all the elements of the sea in their home, from old-world lanterns and playful tin buckets to bowls of delicate starfish and sand dollars.

ABOVE: A shabby-chic bedroom is all romance and frills. The ruffled bedding drapes decadently onto the floor. Rows of oversize pillows speak to comfort first. The beadboard trim provides a crisp hit of pure white that helps sharpen your focus on the light blue-green walls. A French-style chandelier makes sense as the perfect finishing touch.

OPPOSITE: A big bath is the ultimate luxury. To have one with so much natural light is even more spectacular. The freestanding tub is almost sculptural, and acts as the focal point of the room. With a cool, marble-tiled floor and simple bench, the bath is a true escape. In a house typically full of people, this has the added benefit of providing for some wonderful alone time.

OPPOSITE: In my estimation, the nicest time of day on the shore is early evening. When you are lucky enough to have a house right on the beach, it's so easy to get everyone out on the sand. The LaBelles take maximum advantage of their location by enjoying this outdoor time with family.

SURPRISE

If you go through life only experiencing the predictable and the everyday, things can get pretty boring. Luckily, living on the coast has a cure for the ordinary—the ocean is constantly changing, and with every breeze comes something fresh and new. Beach houses often contain elements of surprise and excitement. After all, these are the homes where we come to play by the sea. Here, we tend to be more relaxed, open to new experiences, and curious about our surroundings.

Have you ever noticed that your heart beats faster at the promise of something unexpected? What's around that corner? Or just outside that window? Curiosity pushes us to seek out the unknown because it is mentally stimulating. This intellectual engagement in the world has far-reaching benefits. The best houses take us to interesting places by exciting us, energizing us. They leave their visual gifts to be discovered like a wonderful trail of breadcrumbs.

Mae West once famously said, "Those who are easily shocked should be shocked more often." Very funny, and very true! She would be proud of the risks taken in this chapter. One house reignites childhood fantasies with girly chandeliers and tie-dye-inspired curtains. Another boasts a giant chalkboard for creative expression. And a Caribbean retreat plays games with us, from faux rugs stenciled on the floors to a sofa that hangs from the ceiling.

Playful touches like these draw us in. When you feed your curiosity and take some decorating risks, you can add a lot of fun to your life.

CREATIVE THINKING
Venice, California

WHEN LIFE GIVES YOU LEMONS, MAKE lemonade—preferably at a beach cottage in a breezy California town. This was the driving force behind one homeowner's quest to find happiness in her new home, and the main reason why I just had to include her story in my book.

A few years ago, just about everything seemed to be a challenge for actress Katherine LaNasa. She was an empty-nester, her 11-year marriage had just ended, and her son's father was seriously ill. "I found myself starting over," she tells me. She moved out of her 5,200-square-foot Georgian-style home in Beverly Hills and located a small bungalow for herself in Venice. Once there, she wondered: Can a house heal you? Based on the conversations I have had with people about their beach houses, I can safely say that I think it can.

To answer that question for herself, LaNasa tells me she vowed to take control of the one thing she could: her environment. She began to decorate her new cottage with a purpose, filling it with surprises that feel like little gifts throughout. "I had to decide to be happy," she says. And so she decreed that the spaces in her home would be cheerful, with the hope that the optimistic feelings she created there would soon rub off on her.

Did it work? Big time.

LaNasa's particular cocktail for happiness comes from an unexpected blend of French beach posters from the 1920s and '30s; an abundance of orange, turquoise, and yellow; lots of Art Deco items; a handful of kitschy travel souvenirs; and one extraordinary butterfly wall hanging from Costa Rica. It's all knit together in a surprising mix of color, pattern, and texture. The result: Nothing about this house is routine or boring. Every item comes with a memory, from the hula dancer posed on the coffee table to the Moroccan throw pillow and the orange chair.

The unpredictable combination of these items lends a sense of fun to the house. Was LaNasa ever worried about how things would match here? Well, maybe just a little bit. "It is a good idea to at least have a color scheme," she tells me. "You just can't get too tight about it, or it will end up looking like a hotel." Sometimes we can get so hung up on decorating mandates (only display objects in groups of three, for example), that we miss opportunities to be creative. I find that much of the beauty of a beach house lies in its quirkiness. Hotel rooms can of course be beautiful, but they cannot be personal. Looking at this house, I can see LaNasa playing fast and loose with the decor, mixing and matching in ways that feel a little wrong in all the right ways. That's the element of surprise that defines the happiness quotient in this romantic cottage.

Much of the reason her house tickles my funny bone is thanks to its playful accessories. "You can't take yourself too seriously when drinking out of a mai tai glass. Life seems pretty good then," she says. So true! Looking on the bright side is a wonderful way to live. She tells me that her lamp even has a page from a book that says, "Most problems can be fixed by turning it off and turning it back on again." It all spells happy with a capital H.

All of the items in the house are relevant to its owner; they may have come from one of her travels, or they may contain special memories. It adds a happy spirit to a house to include things that mean something to you. To that end,

OPPOSITE: The curtains in the living room are custom dyed several shades of blue reminiscent of the ocean. The informal, hippie, tie-dye look is then incongruously paired with formal pleats and lined fabric. Just because things aren't supposed to go together, doesn't mean they can't. There is an impish joy in breaking the rules to such good effect.

she lets me know that she rarely throws anything away. "I like to reuse things," LaNasa says. "I decorate by moving them around and painting things and finding new places for them. There is not a lot of soul in the new," she says.

But even with so many different memories, time periods, and travel souvenirs, I find the jumbled result surprisingly pleasing and even thematic. Therein lies the beauty of this house. "If you allow yourself to do things on the fly, sometimes it comes out better," LaNasa tells me. This is a nice concept because it encourages freedom, and I must bear this in mind the next time I find myself spending too long making a decorating decision.

The breakfast table, a treasured flea market find, was renewed with a coat of aqua lacquer paint and placed near a vibrant oversize painting of Louis Armstrong by New Orleans folk artist Nilo Lanza. The unexpected is at work here. Even in such a small space, there are constant discoveries as you move through the rooms: a laminate floor painted bright blue, mismatched cane chairs, coral-painted shelving in the kitchen to show off a collection of Fiestaware, and a Parisian-style chandelier in the casual dining room. It's OK to take risks. The chandelier is a big piece that hangs low above a small table. An unusual combination, to be sure, but it works. "No one ever thinks it looks too big or too low or too anything!" she tells me. Large-scale items in small spaces are just one more way to expand the ooh factor throughout a cottage.

"Our minds like to be challenged, and we like to be surprised visually," LaNasa says. "The beautiful things that are unexpected always give joy." The statement doesn't have to be big. Something as simple as yellow tulips in a blue vase is immediately satisfying. Every time you walk into the room and see it, your brain registers positive feelings.

Looking back now, LaNasa tells me that the house was the beginning of many good things. Perhaps she has even proven to us all that a house can indeed have the power to kickstart happiness. She has since moved and begun a new life elsewhere. "So many wonderful things happened to me after I had that house. I fell in love. I got married. And I had a baby." Her acting career is blooming, too. From lemons came plenty of sweet lemonade. "Whatever you put into your home, your home gives back to you," she tells me. I thank her for reminding me of that.

ABOVE: The homeowner broadcasts optimistic feelings in her happy-face T-shirt. Behind her, artfully arranged treasures from her journeys around the world are reminders that life is good. The decorating surprises continue with a light, frilly shade atop a heavy, twisted lamp base.

OPPOSITE: The galley kitchen bubbles over with happy surprises, from the 3-D watermelon art above the cheerfully curtained windows to the coral-and-white striped rug on the floor. Dramatically contrasting black tile and cabinets below keep things sleek and cool.

OPPOSITE: Where some would hang a single painting, LaNasa finds room for a dozen, mixing mediums and styles—some framed, and some unframed. Like most beach lovers, she adores shells and finds plenty of spots to showcase them, from baskets to shelves. The whole display is a conversation starter, to be sure. I'm ready with a million questions, starting with that well-used artist's palette and the wonderful antique elephant.

ABOVE: LaNasa commandeered this space, which was too small to serve as a guest bedroom, as a walk-in closet. In a tiny cottage, a large dressing room is a rare luxury. The chandelier adds *a je ne sais quoi* that is perfectly at home in this private area.

OPPOSITE: You can't have too many chandeliers! Such a grand statement in a small space sends a little ripple of pleasure. Who wouldn't want to sit beneath it at this rustic Parisian-style table with its sweet red-and-white striped chairs?

TREASURE HUNTING

Treasure Beach, Jamaica

THERE ARE SURPRISES AROUND EVERY CORNER at Sophie Eyssautier's house in Treasure Beach, Jamaica. I notice right away that the sofa doesn't just sit on the floor like any ordinary piece of furniture; it swings from the ceiling. The doorways are not straightforward architectural elements, hung at right angles; they are wonderfully curvaceous Moroccan-style passageways. And the wall in the dining area is not simply painted white; it is hand-drawn with a delightful mural of coral branches, spreading upward from the floor like an actual living thing. These are the details that make me look, and look again.

In fact, the whole house appears to be changing before my very eyes, as a living, breathing example of design in process. Houses can be like that. They can grow with you. In fact, Eyssautier tells me she is never fully satisfied with the way things are. A French fashion designer and artist, she continually moves pieces around and makes changes, adding layers of excitement to her little home by the sea. "It is a constant evolution," she says. Because there was no master plan, sometimes the house surprises even its creator, who says she allows the decor to grow organically. She continues to give herself the freedom to move in different directions and try new things. "The longer I live here, the more I see what I can do," she tells me. So she adds to it, always thinking she can do better. Too often we decorate with an end goal in mind and forget that our interiors do not have to remain frozen in time. Constantly tweaking a design frees us to have more fun with our decor.

More than anything, I can see that the design of the house reflects Eyssautier's personality, moods, and history, including style elements from Greece, the Caribbean,

Morocco, and more. People are complex and multifaceted—they bring a lot of memories with them when they move into a house, and there are ways to honor that without leaving any of it behind. When I ask Eyssautier how the unexpected elements in her house lead to happiness, she tells me that she simply strives to do all the things she loves. If that creates a big mix of things, then so be it. I instantly understand what she is saying. "Mixing cultures makes me happy," she tells me. Add to this melting pot the discerning eye of an artist and you understand the motives behind the lively juxtaposition.

Then she tells me something that many people with beach houses say: "This is my dream house." But she adds something that I don't always hear—a level of complete contentment. "Everything I have ever dreamed of, I have here," she says. And I realize that this is what I love about her house and why I wanted to write about it. It has layers that invite you to discover things about the owner. It is like music, and there are multiple notes and chords being played. If, like Eyssautier, you want to bring competing global styles into the same house, embrace them openly in every room. Trying to separate them would be like playing a single note. Together the individual notes become a beautiful orchestral arrangement.

Perhaps the biggest revelation of all for Eyssautier is how her guests react when they visit her home. She tells me that she thought she was being very selfish while decorating. "I just thought about me," she says. "It was never about pleasing anyone else. So I am so surprised by how much everyone likes what I've done. I didn't expect this reaction." Friends tell her that the house makes them feel comfortable and instantly happy, like a warm embrace from someone they know well. In expressing

OPPOSITE: You learn to expect the unexpected in this Caribbean retreat, with its eclectic mix of decorative elements. A coral mural spreads out across a smooth white wall, turning the dining nook into a work of art. I love the whimsical orange wire chairs with their wooden seats—yet another enjoyable surprise. And the faux runner going up the steps is a delight.

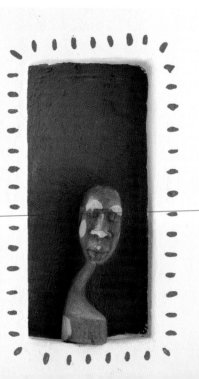

their happiness with it, her friends are clearly affirming their affection not just for the house, but for her.

I don't have to look far to see where Eyssautier's wonderful sense of imagination comes from. "I used to love playing dress up as a child," she tells me, and I can see that she brings that same playful spirit to decorating. There is a joy in what she does that is akin to child's play, full of cheerful abandon and a disregard for the rules. The concrete floor sports a faux rug. The bedroom wall wears a dress of sea urchins. The stairwell features jaunty green cactus leaves hanging on the wall at regular intervals, like fanciful feathers in its cap. I find it all delightful.

Things come to Eyssautier from her travels, from her reading, even from her walks on the beaches of Jamaica. She tells me she had seen stones used as a decorating motif on a wall in Mexico. Then one day while she was walking her dog on the beach, she saw the urchins that are now on her bedroom wall. "I began to collect them day after day on my walks," she reports. She turned them into a focal point in the bedroom by deciding to first paint one wall of the room bright yellow. The white urchins pop off the wall like polka dots. There are many things in Eyssautier's house that seem to be there for no other purpose than to put a smile on your face. If something is pretty and makes you feel happy, that is reason enough to have it in your house.

Sometimes we don't know if something will work until we try it. The nice thing about beach houses is that we all tend to be a little more free here, more willing to push the boundaries and be creative. Will it work to combine airy and colorful wire chairs with a heavy cedar table? Will it look good to mix wood and concrete in the kitchen? Why not try? I agree with Eyssautier that these are risks worth taking. In fact I took her lessons to heart recently

and paired antique wooden chairs with a modern glass-and-wood round table in my kitchen.

I like the result but now I am thinking about scraping the chairs down and painting them white. Eyssautier's house reminds me that change is good. Letting your house "fill out a little" around you can lead to happy places. So I am putting the chairs on this summer's to-do list. Surprising yourself (and others) is just plain fun, because the result is almost always entertaining. Yes, it can shake you up to make swaps and switches, but if done the right way, it's like a roller coaster: a little thrilling. When people enter Eyssautier's house, she tells me that they always say, "Wow! I love it! I never would have thought of doing that!" That's something I want to hear, too.

Eyssautier ends our conversation the way it began, marveling at other people's reactions—including mine, for I make no secret of how enchanting I find it all. "I'm telling you, it's a very strange feeling," she says. But she realizes that this element of surprise is the key to its success. The various elements work because each one of them comes from the same place: the homeowner's sheer love of it. "I guess when you do something with your heart, it shows."

PREVIOUS PAGE: The living room is bright and bohemian, with a hanging sofa piled high with pillows. The leather poufs are from Marrakech. A menagerie of creatures—including a 3-D elephant, a wooden fish, and a portrait of a dog—captures the imagination.

ABOVE: The kitchen mixes wood and concrete, an unusual pairing that turns out to be a fine fit for the home. Natural and organic materials feel right here. Two wire-and-wood stools at the island provide an easy perch for snacking.

OPPOSITE: A collection of decorative elements and architectural extras shows off the exuberant style of this beach house. Paintings, sculptures, and everyday items blend with wonderful colors—so fitting in the home of an artist.

PREVIOUS PAGE: I'm a sucker for bright, lemon-drop yellow, one of the happiest shades on the planet. And here it tells a wonderful bedtime story. But what works so well is that the color is used judiciously on only one wall, set off by white urchins that twinkle like stars.

ABOVE: Pale blues in the bath have a calming effect. The sink, with unadorned faucets coming straight from the wall, is a smooth, simple concrete fixture. A bamboo ladder serves as a towel rack. It all feels very Caribbean until the Moorish passageways take you out of this world.

OPPOSITE: Two butterfly chairs on the terrace are nicely positioned for taking in the outstanding view. The surprise here is on the cement floor—a stencil that gives the appearance of a throw rug. Faux and fabulous! A fringed pendant above has real island style.

EACH DAY BY THE SEA HOLDS SURPRISES—
THE UNEXPECTED CAN BE BEAUTIFUL

THE WOW FACTOR
San Clemente, California

NOW HERE IS A HOUSE THAT TOOK COURAGE and imagination to build! It is a great example of the joy that we get out of being surprised and challenged by what we see. This family had no interest in constructing a house that looked like the others in the neighborhood. They had their own ideas, and the piece of land they bought proved to be a wonderful blank slate on which they could draw exciting new lines.

Peggy Dupuis grew up in California, but then moved to Paris, where she lives with her French husband, Richard, and two children. Still, the pull of the West Coast was strong enough that she and her family decided to buy an empty lot in a small private community in San Clemente, California, near Peggy's family. The land was unusually flat for coastal California, located on the highest point in San Clemente with amazing ocean views. Maybe because of the creative and artsy California atmosphere, Peggy felt free to branch out and gave herself permission to move forward with some bold new ideas. The house she built takes people by surprise—and spreads joy like a shiny new toy.

Once the couple knew they planned to go their own way and build something unexpected and exciting, they thought first about how to take advantage of the water views. "We wanted the house to be open with a lot of space and light," Peggy tells me. And they were uniquely suited to the challenge. Given that he is a civil engineer and she is an interior architect and landscape designer, they put their heads together, came up with a rough plan for a glass structure, and then turned it over to their architect, the late Dale Naegle. An open design with lots of natural light was especially important to them because their apartment in Paris is a much more closed-in space. In California, their windowed box of a house was designed to be its polar opposite, so they used mainly steel and lots of glass.

The look they achieved is spectacular and surprising, but still manages to be relaxing, in part because of its laid-back California feel and airy, lounge-like vibe. There are no formal rooms in this house. The pool is for all intents and purposes inside the living room. What inner child wouldn't cry out for this? "We wanted an indoor/outdoor feel," Peggy tells me. "It's like the pool comes right into the house." Meanwhile, the furniture mimics the whimsy of the architecture. The coffee table is oval-shaped, like an eye. The rug has the same contours but is geometric.

But one of the most striking features of this contemporary stunner is the interior staircase. It is the feature that stopped me in my tracks when I first saw the house. "Friends have said it looks like the backbone of a whale," Peggy tells me. In a way, it does, located as it is in the center of the house. Its graceful arch and lack of risers make it virtually see-through. "We really wanted it to curve and not be straight and angular. We wanted to be able to see it from everywhere, and we wanted it to be transparent." I love that it can be so modern and still evoke the majesty of nature and remind people of a whale. If there were any thought that modern means cold, it would end here.

The house is a standout in the neighborhood, not just because of its modern, square shape but also because of its statement-making front door, framed by a red band— a visual thunderbolt among all that glass, steel, and white

OPPOSITE: It's all about the view at this contemporary stunner on the California coast. Natural light streams into the house thanks to floor-to-ceiling aluminum-framed windows. The white exterior stands in relief against an incredibly blue California sky. And it looks like the pool is being invited right into the living room.

wood. Here and there throughout the house are architectural and design moments that go "poof!" It's as though you are watching a magician pull things from his hat. The enormous blackboard wall upstairs encourages shared now-you-see-it, now-you-don't creativity. "Our guests get a little crazy over this board," Peggy tells me. "No one ever wants it to be erased."

Peggy was exacting in her pursuit of visual excitement. She even had the colored concrete floor hand-troweled by an expert from France. She tells me that this floor now feels to her like she is walking on clouds. I love this description. It reminds me that when our homes truly speak to who we are, they can be like a little piece of heaven.

Upstairs, she was equally precise about the walls. "The paint has a sand base and pearl powder. I mixed the color myself to get that red." Ever the interior design magician, she explains to me that using a strong red against the white optically brings the wall closer to the water. But she has another trick up her sleeve: The wall of her bedroom is curved and, following that shape, the bed is round. Although I have to admit I wonder about the difficulty of buying sheets for it, I can appreciate the magic at work. The wallpaper is from France, and it is magnificent and not the least bit expected: cherry blossoms on a black background. I am not sure I would be brave enough to try black wallpaper but it just goes to show that in the right hands, even the most daring choices can succeed. Note to self: Loosen up a little!

Peggy tells me the French word for surprising: *étonnant,* a good thing that makes life worth celebrating—like a great birthday party. So it is fitting that this house has kept on giving to the family. They use it as a part-time home, but Peggy also works here when she is in town. In love with the space and the view, she tells me that she thinks they accomplished everything they were hoping for: "We wanted that wow factor!" And wow, that's exactly what they got.

OPPOSITE: In the airy living room, ceilings and walls seem almost superfluous. Chrome legs on the low coffee table and matching black side chairs paired with a white sofa increase the visual lightness of the room. But the biggest surprise of all comes from the dramatic sweep of steps reminiscent of the backbone of a whale. They maintain the thread of openness and transparency that defines this house.

ABOVE: Built-in bookshelves on the upstairs landing hold all the things beach houses are rightly famous for—good books, photos, vases, and starfish—but it also houses some surprises, like the primitive masks displayed as sculptures.

OPPOSITE: The homeowners' daughter sits in a red butterfly chair in front of a chalkboard wall, which provides a happy playground for creative thoughts and sentiments. At the same time, it neatly reinforces the modern palette of black, white, and gray used throughout the home.

ABOVE: The wallpaper behind the bed is from France. With its fluffy white cherry blossoms bursting across a black background, it is unique, charming, and out of the ordinary. The woven look adds texture and brightness. All-white bedding on a round bed and a white end table enhance the dream.

OPPOSITE: The off-white contemporary home gets an exciting punctuation mark with a tall red panel at the front entrance. A pretty light wood door with an aluminum band maintains the simple, modern lines. The landscaping keeps greenery low and neat so as not to distract from the architecture of the house.

NATURE

External cues—the feel of smooth pebbles on a beach, the smell of a freshly mown lawn, the sound of wind moving through a beautiful beech tree—can affect our emotions in profound ways. Many of us know intuitively that time with nature improves our disposition. The sun shining on cresting waves or a hike along a cliff as the stresses of the day begin to fade are moments that make us feel good. And science is now confirming what we have long known in our hearts: Proximity to nature can increase feelings of well-being. It's important to our health.

The simple act of viewing nature helps to decrease stress levels, and coastal views are particularly powerful. Why do you think so many people have beach scenes as their screen savers at work? We are drawn to the restful, restorative magic that the sea works on us. Even small reminders of nature can help. In my office, I keep a bowl of shells on a table and a row of starfish along the windowsill. Although I have no view of the water, I feel happier and more connected to the beach.

Beach houses, of course, sit on the front row of this important philosophy thanks to the way they welcome the outdoors in—whether that means a home on land that backs up against a nature preserve, a rustic stone cottage that cozily protects its occupants from the sea winds, a Caribbean retreat with virtually no walls at all, or a compound that relies on a patchwork of tents, shacks, and decks to make nature the main decorative element.

Whenever I need a pick-me-up, just seeing pictures of these outstanding properties is all I need. When I look at them, I can't help but smile.

OUT AND ABOUT
Savary Island, British Columbia

WHAT GREATER HAPPINESS CAN THERE be than to be surrounded by beauty, with time to sleep, read, relax, and truly enjoy the outdoors? The connection between the human psyche and nature is still being explored, but this much we do know: The environment affects our emotions in a positive way. The pounding of the ocean, the rustle of the leaves, the quiet swaying of long green grasses in a meadow, the feel of a piece of drift-wood in your hand—these are the healing sights, sounds, and sensations that center and de-stress us. And these are the things April and Alec Tidey experience every day at their rustic home on Savary Island in British Columbia, where they unwind and reboot in the summers.

The Tideys have been coming here for 10 years now, and the amazing view is the magnet. From their position on this bluff, they can see far and wide, across the gorgeous Georgia Strait to Vancouver Island, which gives them an enviable sense of calm and stability. Exposure to nature is an easy way to clear our heads and to put things in proper perspective. The Tideys are a testament to that notion. April tells me that arriving here immediately brings her blood pressure down. That's the way it should be with a beach house. And a house that is so well connected to nature likely has twice the effect!

Looking at this bucolic island, it is easy to see what attracted the Tideys. "When I stood on the bluff that first time, I knew this was it. It took my breath away, and it still does every single time I see it," April tells me. It's the type of view that one wants to inhale. As you walk toward the edge of the bluff, the vista just continues to open up. Here, you can watch the tides change. The beauty of the

location meant that the couple had to work hard not to disturb the setting with overbearing architecture. They knew that outdoor spaces would be the most important.

On a heavily forested island, their site is a big, open, grassy area. So they began by constructing a deck at the edge of the bluff, thinking that the new house they wanted to build would sit directly behind it. Apparently good things really do come to those who wait, because by moving slowly with their plans, they had time to think and reassess their needs and desires. It became clear to the Tideys over time that the humble fisherman's shack already sitting on the property—a 500-square-foot Pan-Abode structure from 1948—might be all they really needed.

Well, almost all. An additional shack (purchased from a neighbor) was added later, as well as a prospector tent from The Kerrisdale Lumber Co. The three structures are now connected by weathered gray wood decking, creat-ing a wonderful compound of rustic dwellings that feels right at home in the setting and is a draw for family and friends. With prime spots for taking in the view as well as dining and hanging out, this family truly found their hearts' desire right here. And they were able to preserve the grassy meadow that they loved so much.

Of course, changes had to be made. The little shack was dark, had no real kitchen, and was lacking in windows and views. It was really no more than a place for an angler to lay his head at night after a full day of fishing. The Tideys also enjoy clamming, prawning, and fishing, but when they come home now it is to a much more open and airy indoor space. They took a chain saw and skill saw to the walls, and cut a hole in the bedroom to gain access to the outside and to create bigger views. Now it is a wonder-fully inviting and bright home with windows that open

OPPOSITE: The living room windows in the main house open wide to the breezes. The color palette blends in nicely with the tall grasses just outside. Furnishings are simple, an easy grouping of midcentury-modern items that look as though they have been collected over time. The rattan seating speaks to the charm of natural materials.

to let the air in. "I leave them open all day," April says. "You can always get a good breeze." The simple floor plan and vaulted ceilings remain.

Much of what is in the house came from outside: pieces of driftwood from the beach, reclaimed wood, and rocks and shells found along the shore. The hand-hewn benches on the deck were built on site. Like all good nature lovers, the Tideys are happy scavengers. Treasures you find on the beach can easily become part of your decor, especially if you have a little imagination. Driftwood can become a shelf, wood from a fallen tree can serve as an end table, a perfectly round rock can become a piece of art. Collect things that appeal to you. A lot of creativity can come from using the found objects that catch your eye.

I love that everything here enhances the connection to the outdoors. The Tideys find that they always eat outside; the main dining table is outdoors. The walls are painted white to reflect the light and to contrast the incredible blue of the summer skies. Furnishings inside the shacks are simple, functional, and unpretentious. The space is comfortable and uncluttered. It suits the fishing shack sensibility as well as a pair of old jeans. But before you think this house is overly utilitarian, look closer. Beautiful antique French linen tablecloths are on the daybed, adding a touch of refined elegance to the unassuming surrounds. I like it when certain items are used in different ways than originally intended. Instead of being put into service on a fussy dining table, the cloths have been turned into cozy coverlets, allowing a wonderful blend of formality and a casual, relaxed approach to island life.

For the Tideys, this spot is about enjoying nature, and the goal is ultimate relaxation. April tells me about a typical day, one that she is able to repeat often during summer months: "I sit on the bluff deck in the morning with my coffee, reading an entire newspaper from front to back with the sun to warm me. In the evening I am back again with my tea and chocolate." Not a bad day to put on instant replay!

The physical relationship with nature adds to the happy state of mind the homeowners regularly find them-selves in. A good long walk, a fishing trip, a delicious meal, a quiet cup of tea, or an intimate conversation: These are the things in life that give us energy and rejuvenate us. And they are the stock and trade of this unassuming home on an achingly beautiful Pacific Northwest island.

ABOVE: A classic Saarinen tulip table in the kitchen is a triumph of clean lines and is surrounded by Eames molded fiberglass chairs. Together, they create a stylish corner for enjoying breakfast before heading outside.

OPPOSITE: Wherever you look, there are small shrines to the great outdoors. A few gathered stalks of tall grass are placed in a glass bottle, some round rocks sit on a shelf, and a piece of dark wood acts as artful sculpture. All of it reminds you to slow down and appreciate life.

ABOVE: A prospector tent from The Kerrisdale Lumber Co. is used for guests. I never would have thought of a tent as an extra bedroom, but it works perfectly! It reminds me of the glamping experiences so popular at nature sites throughout the world.

OPPOSITE: The comfortably wrinkled sectional sofa is created from two beds pushed together to form an L shape. The wall art is an interesting assortment of meaningful objects, including vintage postcards and black-and-white photos. The feeling is rustic and lived-in. A Dutch door adds to the cabin's charm.

ABOVE: White butterfly chairs offer easy, camp-style seating. A wooden bench running the length of the windows is a natural place for a collection of found objects brought back from the family's daily walks. The reedy cushions thrown on the deck for extra seating are from a drugstore.

OPPOSITE: The dramatic view from this high perch is what first captured the couple's attention and drew them to purchase the property. The beauty of it has never lost its hold on them. To create some shade for the exposed area, they hung triangular nylon sails from driftwood poles, lending the deck an organic feel—the sails look more like billowy clouds than tenting.

INSIDE OUT

Stinson Beach, California

WITH THE GOLDEN GATE NATURAL Recreation Area peaks on one side and the Pacific Ocean on the other, this is a house that is embraced by nature in a big way. I chose it for this book because I feel it represents an unusually open approach to its surroundings. A single-story home like this one, arranged around a courtyard, has an inclusive feel that invites those outside to step in, and those inside to step out. The two arms of the house seem to reach out to hug the world. Conceived of as a family house, it was built on a lot that the homeowners' grandmother bought in 1950. For decades, the plan had been to develop the land and create a family retreat—surrounded by the best Mother Nature has to offer, but doing nothing to disrupt the scenery, allowing the beach to run all the way to the base of the mountains as it has done for hundreds of years.

Although 35 years passed before the plan could be enacted, it fortuitously came to fruition under the watchful eye of Lewis Butler, the property owner's very own grandson, who had by then become an architect. With a footprint of around 2,000 square feet, it leaves its mark, but it does so quietly. A stone courtyard faces the mountains, with lush landscaping that hides the view of the street. This is an excellent architectural and landscaping approach; you don't see the other roads or the other houses, which has the benefit of making the house seem to be alone amid the sand dunes. Opposite the courtyard, the indoor living room doubles as an outdoor living room, thanks to matching nine-pane windows flanking the space and big sliding doors that open to the sand. The beach

is stunningly beautiful, one of the major calling cards of the Stinson Beach community.

In deference to the site, everything about the house is purposely open to the natural surroundings. With no air-conditioning, this free-flowing arrangement is especially important: Breezes can pass right through the rooms, cooling them down on those few days when Stinson Beach thermometers climb past the 80-degree mark. The dune grass grows right up to the back deck. The deck is only about 14 feet deep, essentially pushing you out onto the sand, to the conveniently placed Adirondack chairs and beyond. A covered porch on the side of the house allows for playing Ping-Pong in the rain, so even inclement weather doesn't stop you from living an active outdoor life.

"I am tremendously happy here," Butler tells me. "The house is only 45 minutes away, but everything just washes away as soon as I arrive." This is the trick of beach houses; no matter how close they may be to your primary residence, they feel a world apart, and troubles can be left behind.

The outdoor shower is just one of the many things about this home that help further that goal. It has rightly become everyone's favorite spot. It's a place to breathe more deeply and have a sense that life's possibilities are so much greater. Perhaps I am putting an awful lot of philosophical weight on the outdoor shower, but I don't think so. After a day of sand and sea, it is wonderfully restorative and refreshing.

The home's interior is designed to channel the peaceful feelings that come with being close to nature. From the subtle, sea-inspired colors to the comfortable weatherproof fabric, everything is in keeping with the location. The roller shades in the bedroom disappear into spaces above the

OPPOSITE: In the den, good books and a stunning sea view are both easily accessed. The comfortable sectional sofa is actually composed of two twin beds, covered in custom fabric and dressed with throw pillows. A glass bowl of shells on the round coffee table is a reminder of the nature that surrounds the house.

windows. The house exudes a back-to-basics feeling. Even the light fixtures are unadorned. Frosted bare bulbs illuminate the house from the ceiling rafters, casting a flattering glow, like Hollywood dressing room lights. The seatbelt chairs and Aalto Finnish coffee table are hits of midcentury modern that keep the house feeling modest and light. The open-stud walls give the home a slightly unfinished look, as though the carpenters stopped midway, too pleased with their work so far to continue. Shell collections gather organically on the ledges created by the wood framing. "The house is meant to feel like you are outside even when you are inside," Butler tells me.

A good beach house is humble in that way; its beauty is dependent on the beauty around it. Only by letting that shine can it truly shine. This house respects the natural setting and doesn't impose itself. It lets the real splendor of the place take center stage: the beach, the mountains, the ocean. Butler's family dreamed of being together under one roof in a place where they could enjoy the company not only of nature but also of each other—and that fantasy has been realized. The house boasts an uncomplicated elegance that allows generations to come together and celebrate their love for the great outdoors. The happiness that comes from that experience is intangible.

A tribute to Butler's grandparents sits on the hearth next to the woodstove fireplace. It's a board from their Santa Cruz house, with a Latin inscription that reads *"Tuum est."* Loosely translated, that means "It is up to you." It's a simple sentiment that can be understood a number of different ways. But Butler tells me that for him, it signifies that happiness is yours to discover, and life is what you make it. Which is made all that much easier to embrace in a place where what you hear is the crashing of the sea, the cries of the seabirds, and the laughter of your family.

OPPOSITE: Balanced and meticulously proportioned, the architecture is deliberately reminiscent of a 1930s Santa Cruz house built for the homeowners' grandparents by architect William Wurster. A pioneer of the ranch house style known for blurring the lines between indoors and out, Wurster's work proved to be the perfect inspiration.

ABOVE: The windowed doors fully retract so that you can look straight through the house, from the mountains to the beach. The curtains can also be drawn back into pockets so that they completely tuck away, leaving no barriers to the outdoors.

OPPOSITE: Nature is honored indoors by the subdued color palette. The living room hues are all grays and light blues, like the ocean, and the fir floors are stained to match the color of the dunes. The rug purposely mimics the restful shades of sea and sky.

ABOVE: The serene and uncluttered bedroom is softened by the use of many interesting textiles, including a white quilted bedspread and beaded pillow. A blue-and-white Persian jajim textile hangs behind the bed in lieu of a headboard. The white lamp and wooden nightstand make the basics beautiful.

OPPOSITE: The large, gated rinsing station is positioned so that bathers can stand and stare at the ocean. The homeowner says he hasn't used the indoor shower here in years. I don't blame him. Being able to feel the sun and air on your skin while looking at the sky and taking in the view is heavenly.

THE HOUSE WITH NO WALLS

Scrub Island, British Virgin Islands

I CALL THIS "THE HOUSE WITH NO WALLS," ALTHOUGH in reality it does have a few. You just tend to forget about them when you are here, with the sun shining in, the fragrant breezes blowing, and the unobstructed view everywhere you look. The house sits on a high bluff overlooking the Atlantic Ocean and the Caribbean Sea on Scrub Island in the British Virgin Islands, and it is as close to nature as you can get without a sleeping bag. "There is a big difference between hearing the sounds of the waves amidst other sounds and hearing no sound at all except the waves," owner Davide Pugliese tells me, and I think this is an important distinction. It is not something most people get the chance to experience, certainly not on a daily basis as he and his wife, Cele, do.

The Puglieses were inspired by the feeling of being on a boat. They wanted to experience the sun, wind, and sea all the time, even when at home. Davide tells me that there is a term for people like him who need to be surrounded by water to be happy. Hydrophilia, I wonder? Thalassophilia? I know that the former refers to a love of water, and the latter to a love of the sea. But he introduces me to a new word: islaphilia, which he says is the need to be *surrounded* by water. Island life is the only cure!

Because I share that passion for the water, I was thrilled to be able to see a house that almost completely erases the dividing line between life indoors and life at sea. Davide and Cele coordinated the construction of their dream home— an open-air, two-bedroom, 4,200-square-foot structure— on a dramatic cliffside perch above the sea to optimize the proximity to paradise. Although you enter through a heavy wooden front door, you needn't bother yourself with many others after that. It's like walking inside to get outside—a paradox that's a Robinson Crusoe dream come true ... but without any of those pesky hardships. In some ways, it is the most elaborate tree house I ever could have imagined.

A home that is so intertwined with nature brings an immediate feeling of peace, serenity, and solitude to its occupants—including all the wonderful, romantic parts of being a castaway. Does it ever feel too alone? Too quiet? "If there's ever too much peace, I just crank up the music!" Davide tells me. (Luckily he had the foresight to think ahead and install a sound system throughout his magical retreat.) The living room, dining room, and kitchen are all separated by levels, not by walls. Not only does this keep you connected to the view and to nature, it keeps you connected to other people in the house. "I can be in the kitchen and still have a conversation with someone in the living room," Davide tells me. This is key—as a professional chef, he spends most of his time in the kitchen.

Because the house is so open to the elements, Davide and Cele were particular about the types of furniture they needed. Their main concern? Strong trade winds could knock something over, or even blow it away. No worries here: The massive dining room table, for example, is made of very dense wood and is one solid piece. Hearing Davide tell stories of the challenges inherent in constructing this escape, it becomes clear that everything was a struggle to deliver, a struggle to put in place, and, above all, a struggle to lift or move. There's nothing in his house that isn't heavy. "But none of it is going anywhere now!" he tells me. The

OPPOSITE: Two deck chairs from Bali face out to sea and overlook the pool. This is a magical place. It seems appropriate, in a house surrounded by water, for this couple to also build a pool that mimics their island position and allows you to sit surrounded by water. The travertine flooring stays cool, and the billowy drapes provide just the right amount of shade.

solid nature of the house helps me feel safe and protected in spite of the openness. It doesn't hurt that the house is also well stocked with an oversize pantry, walk-in refrigerator, and walk-in freezer. This is, after all, an island—provisions must be considered in advance and kept on hand in the event of storms or other events that disrupt your ability to get more supplies. "I always have a case of olive oil in there," Davide tells me. "And a case of wine!"

It all adds to the fantasy that the house, and nature, can provide everything you need. Fans hang from the ceiling, but are rarely used thanks to the constant breeze. Rainwater is filtered for use, and water is conserved. And so the home's name makes perfect sense: Wali Nikiti is an Australian phrase that means "Bare Hut." In that pure, self-contained simplicity lies its natural beauty.

But although Mother Nature can be kind, she can also be cruel. How does a house as open to the elements as this one protect itself? The house is designed to let wind and water pass through it. But the Puglieses knew they would need added protection from flying debris, so they had tarps made that can hook between the home's pillars. Constructed of a rubberized trampoline material, they shield the interior spaces from incoming objects, which instead bounce right off the house. During light rains and strong sun, roll-down screens instead can offer refuge and shade.

And a refuge it is. I feel as if I could hide away here for a long time and maybe forget that any other world exists. This is exactly as planned, of course, in a house so in tune with nature. It is a magnet for those who wish to escape and unwind: Davide has started hosting private dinner parties for groups of guests arriving by yacht. Unfettered island life is a fantasy that easily becomes a reality at Wali Nikiti. The beauty that surrounds him on this island is unparalleled. Space and solitude are hard won in this day and age, and the Puglieses have found a way to slip into that wonderful space between creature comforts and unbridled, wild, and wonderful nature.

PREVIOUS PAGE: The crowning achievement of the house, its soaring roof, is made of PVC thatch. It's a practical alternative to a traditional thatched roof, which is difficult to maintain and would need to be redressed many times over the years. It looks authentic to me; I would not guess that it was engineered. "You have to touch it to know it's not real," Davide tells me.

ABOVE: In the living area, you have a completely unobstructed view. There are pillars, but no windows or walls, to support the thatched roof. The posts are uniquely suited to the job because they are so dense and strong. In fact, hanging things requires a drill bit—you can't just drive a nail into them! That strength is essential; the beams above weigh 1,200 pounds each.

OPPOSITE: Good food, fresh cocktails, tropical flowers, and beautiful views make life a true paradise for the homeowners and their guests.

ABOVE: The kitchen is the most important part of the house for Davide, who is a gourmet chef renowned throughout the Caribbean. Island solitude is great, but having friends over is part of the fun, too! The concrete center island is big enough for 12 people to sit, watching him prepare the meal. And of course he has a wood-burning pizza oven for parties.

OPPOSITE: Where does this house end and the world begin? It's a question you can sit and ponder over a glass of white wine. Low chairs and soft throw pillows mean that once you've made this spot your perch, you're not likely to get up again anytime soon. The Caribbean Sea stretches out before you, and you're there just to breathe it all in.

AN ISLAND OF ONE'S OWN
Boothbay Harbor, Maine

THERE ARE FEW THINGS MORE ROMANTIC THAN the thought of falling asleep in a cozy stone house on your own forested, one-acre island, with a fire crackling in the fireplace and thick, stacked-stone walls keeping the sea winds at bay. Privacy and rustic beauty combine to make for an incredibly relaxed vacation home in this picturesque corner of Maine. The muted colors, whitewashed stone walls, mahogany windows and doors, and stenciled concrete floors underscore the laid-back allure and warmth at the heart of this house. Completely in tune with nature, the effect is a feeling of serenity, far from the hustle and bustle of everyday life.

One of the words I hear most commonly associated with a beach house is "escape." And there is no better way to describe this tiny island oasis, accessible only by boat. In fact, that's how Bob and Kate Horgan discovered the place, while day-tripping the surrounding seas on their Whaler. As soon as they saw the empty stone cottage, they were smitten and phoned their real estate agent, who suggested they tie up and have a look. The key was in a cooler by the door, and they let themselves in. As they sat inside the house, on a long couch that is still there today, a quiet fell over them. "We felt like we were in church. It was so peaceful, almost spiritual," Kate tells me. By 11 o'clock that night, they had bought it. Sometimes when you fall in love, it happens quickly—especially with beach houses.

Originally built as a hunting lodge, the cottage retains that same casual ambience even though it is now fully renovated with (for the first time!) plumbing and electricity. The Horgans' only connection to the mainland is the electrical wiring that runs underwater. Beyond that, they are very much on their own, and that's the way the couple and their two dogs and cat like it. It is a beautiful thing when a house and its owners are so well matched. Everything about the place keeps them in touch with nature, in ways that positively impact the whole family. The solid stone walls inside echo the rocks outside. Past storms and floods washed away much of the white paint that a previous owner applied to the walls. Rather than repaint, the Horgans left it as-is, appreciating the patina it gives the cottage and respecting the elements that will only continue to weather this house in spite of any efforts to the contrary.

Kate tells me that electrical storms, when they happen, light up the whole house in stunningly brilliant displays of nature's might. And when it is sunny, the rooms are filled with a bright, golden glow. It would be hard not to fall in love with life here. Outside the windows, pine trees bend and sway, partially hiding the path to the nearby guesthouse. The sunsets are spectacular, and often provide the most delightful entertainment. Because the island is so far from the lights of the city, the stars are that much brighter, and the cottage is particularly romantic in the dark.

"We are surrounded by water. The natural elements are so dominant here," Kate tells me. And so they've introduced nature inside the cottage in ways both obvious and subtle. Bringing in these organic touches is a wonderful way to honor their unique location. Above the fireplace hangs a huge mirror framed in driftwood. Kate made the frame herself from wood that washed ashore. Driftwood decor, found in many beach houses, is usually the happy result of what the tides bring in. Gifts from Mother Nature should not be turned down. In the kitchen, antlers are a clear reminder that this used to be a hunting lodge.

The furniture, some Scandinavian in style, is mostly from antiques shops and veers toward the minimal. Items

OPPOSITE: You just know that a cat will find one of the best spots in the house to sit—a sunny, light-filled nook with a beautiful view of the water. Window treatments are noticeably absent here. The home's ultra-private island location (no neighbors!) makes them unnecessary.

ABOVE: The house is designed to stand up to any kind of weather. Because winter flooding could be an issue, there are no carpets or rugs. Instead, a pretty stencil is applied. The rustic stone walls in the dining area are appropriately dressed with landscape paintings.

OPPOSITE: The kitchen is user-friendly, with marble-topped rolling workstations and open shelving. Meals frequently feature fresh Maine lobster, delivered live to the dock and left in a submerged box. When it's dinner-time, the Horgans just go down to the dock and pull it up.

that were purchased were soon deliberately transformed to match the rest of the house. For example, the Horgans left a brand new teak bench outside all winter so that it would weather to the right silvery shade. It is a no-frills approach to island living. Four cane chairs and a love seat are painted white, and the fabric on the latter has a cushion covered with a toile fabric in light blues and browns. Quiet colors do not distract from the scenic views outside and are in keeping with the browns, greens, grays, and blues that are part of the landscape around them. One surprisingly contemporary feature is juxtaposed against the rusticity: track lighting on wires. It provides a practical solution to the Horgans' lighting needs, shining exactly where light is wanted. Better still, the fixtures can be taken down for cleaning. The shades seem almost butterfly-like, adding to the natural elements in the decor.

Not surprisingly, the family loves to share this place with others; they often have family and guests stay with them, and boating neighbors can come for dinner. In this way, they never feel isolated. Unexpected wildlife plays a part in that, as well, for of course they are never truly alone. Birds nest in the trees. Dolphins are sometimes spotted just off shore. And once, the Horgans discovered a baby seal stranded among the rocks. (Happily, they were able to wrap it in a towel and move it to the dock where it could be released into deeper waters. Rescue mission successful!)

In a house built of stones and surrounded by them, it feels appropriate to pay homage to the family's life here with a collection of stones kept in a small, white wooden boat that sits on a table. Unable to resist the call of the smooth rocks scattered along the shore, family and friends often bring them inside, dropping one more into the wooden boat, or placing it on a shelf or on a step. It is a small sign that someone has been here, that footsteps have marked the path to the house, and that fires have been built, lobsters have been eaten, laughter has been shared. Every summer, this cottage provides the Horgans with a connection to a deep need that's within all of us—the need to reconnect with nature and with one another, the need to recharge, and the need to remember what the most important things in our lives are. I think the fact that a little house on a little island can do all that is something of a miracle.

ABOVE: The stair railing includes a long piece of driftwood; sliding your hand along its worn-smooth surface brings back memories of climbing trees as a child. This is one of my favorite parts of the house—I love that the owners rescued this piece from the original cottage and reused it during the renovation.

OPPOSITE: The living room retains an authentic simplicity with a pinstripe ticking chair from Lee Industries. The bench was purchased from an antiques shop in Portland. During the off-season, when storms come and water can rise, the living room furniture is hung from hooks on black wires that stretch across the ceiling. Preparation helps this little cottage to weather the winter after it is closed up for the season.

ABOVE: A claw-foot tub in front of the window means that even while soaking you can keep the outdoors in sight. The windows are trimmed in light blue for a subtle addition of color that complements the striped rug. The retro bath fixtures are from Rohl.

OPPOSITE: The bedroom has plenty of cozy cabin style. Colors are muted, and walls are left undecorated. But a Louis XVI–style upholstered chair, known as a bergère, ups the game. Combined with the decorative antique French mirror and fanciful lamp shade, these pieces lend a Parisian air to the understated room.

NEXT PAGE: Everyone loves to eat outside, with bonfires and votive candles lighting up the dark and turning the home into a luxury campsite, animated by lively tales of the day's adventures.

AT DUSK, **NATURE** DISPLAYS ITS MOST
ROMANTIC SIDE, ENHANCED BY THE WARM GLOW OF A FIRE THAT BRINGS
EVERYONE TOGETHER

ACKNOWLEDGMENTS

Thanks to the entire staff of *Coastal Living* for helping to create a beautiful magazine, without which there could not be a beautiful book. Special thanks to Jennifer Slaton for always giving me such thoughtful direction; to Ellen McGauley for enthusiastically lending her time and abundant skills to this project; to Katie Finley for her patience, smarts, and good humor (and the multiple ways she improved my words); and to Lindsay Lambert Day, Lacie Pinyan, and Diane Keener for all their help. Thanks to designer Lou Dilorenzo for his indefatigable dedication and wonderfully creative ideas. Thanks to Victor Maze, who offered his wise advice. I could not have done this without the amazing Mamie Walling, who keeps everything on track and is our biggest brand cheerleader. Thanks, as well, to my hardworking photo editors, Kristen Fielder and Lindsey Stone, and to all of the talented photographers and stylists whose work appears here. And to Brielle Ferreira, who helped to bring many of these incredible houses to the magazine. I also owe a debt of gratitude to Leah McLaughlin and Felicity Keane for their support and stewardship, and to Sid Evans, who encouraged me to take this book on. And, finally, a great big hug to my whole family, who were forced to read wet, sandy pages of my manuscript while sitting on the beach (when they could have been staring out to sea instead).

DEDICATION

To Peter, Nic, Natalie, Theo, and Tessa—
you make our beach house happy.

CREDITS

INDEX

Photos indicated by bold type.

©2015 by Time Home Entertainment Inc.
1271 Avenue of the Americas, New York, NY 10020

Written by Antonia van der Meer
Designed by Lou Dilorenzo

ISBN-13: 978-0-8487-4429-8
ISBN-10: 0-8487-4429-2
Library of Congress Control Number: 2014953432

Printed in China
First Printing 2015